THE WASTE LAND

A CRITICAL STUDY

THE WASTE LAND

A CRITICAL STUDY

BY

VIKRAMADITYA RAI, M.A., PH.D.

Reader in English, Banaras Hindu University, Varanasi

MOTILAL BANARSIDASS

Delhi Varanasi Patna

Bangalore Madras

First Edition : 1965
Second Edition : 1970
Reprint: 1988

MOTILAL BANARSIDASS
Bungalow Road, Jawahar Nagar, Delhi 110 007

Branches
Chowk, Varanasi 221 001
Ashok Rajpath, Patna 800 004
24 Race Course Road, Bangalore 560 001
120 Royapettah High Road, Mylapore, Madras 600 004

ISBN : 81-208-0537-2

PRINTED IN INDIA
BY JAINENDRA PRAKASH JAIN AT SHRI JAINENDRA PRESS, A-45 NARAINA INDUSTRIAL AREA PHASE I, NEW DELHI 110 028 AND PUBLISHED BY NARENDRA PRAKASH JAIN FOR MOTILAL BANARSIDASS, DELHI 110 007.

To

Dr. R. Dwivedi

With Love and Gratitude

PREFACE

The present book is in the nature of a grateful tribute to the memory of T. S. Eliot whose work has been, to me, a permanent source not only of aesthetic delight but also of intellectual and emotional tonic as well as spiritual consolation for the last fifteen years or so. Thus I owe him a debt which I can best repay by attempting, to the best of my knowledge and critical insight, to make his message and his mastery of the poetic art and craft known to a wide audience of readers and students of literature. The present work is a modest fulfilment of this arduous undertaking and is especially designed to relieve the worry of the post-graduate students of English literature in Indian universities, who have to study *The Waste Land* under compulsion and are hag-ridden with fear of its surface contortions and corrugations, the dragons in the Garden of the modernist Muse.

In the first section of the book an attempt has been made to put together a fairly large number of the representative passages of Eliot's poetry and criticism, together with brief but revealing discussions of all the key poems from *The Love song Of J. Alfred Prufrock* to the *Four Quartets*, which chart out the course of the Poet's progress from early cynicism to his final mysticism. The second section contains an exhaustive analysis of *The Waste Land* in which I have fully availed myself of the help provided by the scholarly critics and interpreters of the poem, to whom I am deeply indebted. But the interpretations of the poem are so divergent and even contradictory that one is apt to lose one's bearings unless one has a definite point of view of one's own. In the most crucial passages, therefore, I have relied on my own light and understanding and offered explanations which, at times, run counter to the received interpretations. I, however, do not presume to dogmatise, and stand open to correction by the enlightened criticism of my readers. The interpretation of the poem is followed by a detailed discussion of the various problems connected with its technique, style and diction, which forms an essential part of the poetic interpretation.

I shall deem my labour amply rewarded if this book lightens the burden of the students and stimulates their interest in the poetry of T. S. Eliot. The book is a fruit of laborious study and prolonged meditation extending for well over 10 years and it is quite in the fitness of things that it should be dedicated to Dr. R. Dwivedi, Hony. Professor of English, Kashi Vidyapeeth, Varanasi, who has been a living inspiration behind whatever I have been able to do or achieve in literature and in life.

V. RAI

B. H. U.
VARANASI
July, 1965.

———

PREFACE TO THE SECOND EDITION

I am glad to offer to the students and teachers of English literature, in India and abroad, the second edition of *The Waste Land: A Critical Study*, as a New year's gift. I am grateful to the discerning students and scholars for the warm and generous reception they have accorded to the volume, which has been commended by an American editor, in a recent publication on Eliot, as 'the only book-length study of the poem.' I have made only minor changes and alterations in the new edition, but have tried my best to rectify the misprints and minor errors which I could discover in the book. I hope this second edition will go a long way towards the removal of all the hurdles which stand in the way of a real understanding and genuine appreciation of a poem, which I, for one, regard as a representative work of the present century and a key to the understanding of modern sensibility and literary technique.

V. RAI

Varanasi,
Dec. 26, 1969.

CONTENTS

SECTION I

SECTION II

SECTION I

THE POETRY OF T. S. ELIOT

THE POETRY OF T. S. ELIOT

For the creation of a master-work in literature two powers must concur, the power of the man and the power of the moment. —Matthew Arnold.

Sensibility alters from generation to generation in everybody whether we will or no, but expression is only altered by a man of genius.—T. S. Eliot.

In the memorial tribute to W. B. Yeats, his great peer in the domain of contemporary literature, Eliot has observed: 'He is one of those few whose history is the history of their own time, who are a part of the consciousness of the age which cannot be understood without them.' One of these fortunate few, it is needless to state, is T. S. Eliot himself, who, while writing himself, also wrote his age and has left behind him a solid output of poetry, criticism and drama, at once individual and idiosyncratic and remarkably representative of the intellectual climate in which he lived and worked. The term 'representative', however, will be misleading if it prompts one to conclude that a poet of this type is a mere recorder of the surface configuration of his society and the ways of living, thinking and feeling, peculiar to the men and women around him.

Eliot's representative capacity is broad-based, because while it rests upon the liveliest awareness of the peculiar nature of the contemporary mind and sensibility, it is, at the same time, frankly assertive of the poet's right to criticize the current modes of thoughts and life; to probe, boldly and unhesitatingly, into the wounds festering in the depth below the surface. Eliot was thus not a mere spokesman of his age, but its gadfly, irritating its complacent mind not unoften, and compelling it, at times, to stop and search its own heart. In his own way he was 'the physician of an iron age', a pitiless exposer of 'the strange disease of modern life, its sick hurry and divided aims, its head overtaxed and its palsied heart' and, one may add, its empty soul:

> The strange time-ridden faces
> Distracted from distraction by distraction
> Filled with fancies and empty of meaning
> Tumid apathy with no concentration
> Men and bits of paper: whirled by the cold wind.

He entered upon the scene of English poetry, an American expatriate of erudite mind and disciplined sensibility, at a time when the Romantic movement of the 19th century and its pale offshoot of the Victorian era, had reached the point of exhaustion and a set of competent observers and intellectual crusaders were militantly insistent upon the necessity of a fresh attempt to re-mould the art and craft of literature in order to make it a suitable medium for the expression of the complex consciousness of this hectic age. Dame Sitwell has put the matter, succinctly and quite clearly, in the preface to her *Collected Poems:*

> 'A change in the direction, imagery, and rhythm in poetry had become necessary owing to the rhythmical flaccidity, the verbal deadness, the dead and expected patterns of some of the poetry immediatey preceding.'

Eliot's passion for discipline in life and literature

naturally led him into the anti-romantic camp, composed of such sturdy and noted figures as Irving Babbitt, Paul Elmer More, T. E. Hulme and Ezra Pound and a set of French critics and artists, whose influence he imbibed and assimilated and candidly acknowledged subsequently.

His poetic creed and formative influences: In *the Music of Poetry*, 1942, Eliot has underscored the essential unity of his critical and creative writings which we should do well to keep constantly in mind in the present section.

> .. ..the critical writings of poets owe a great deal of their interest to the fact that at the back of the poet's mind, if not as his ostensible purpose, he is always trying to defend the kind of poetry he is writing or to formulate the kind that he wants to write. Especially when he is young, and actively engaged in battling for the kind of poetry he practises; he sees the poetry of the past in relation to his own."

It is, therefore, not unreasonable to elaborate his poetic credo and poetic technique, his artistic aims and ideals with the help of suitable citations from his own literary criticism. We shall start with his famous declaration, in 1928, that he was a classicist in literature, a royalist in politics and an Anglo-Catholic in religion. His classicism, in the first place, was a reaction against Romantic subjectivism and emotional excess, in the direction of impersonality, objectivity and the universality of the artistic emotion. He is naturally over-emphatic and even dogmatic in his statements on this point. In '*Tradition and The Individual Talent*', he asserts positively that poetry 'is not a turning loose of emotion but an escape from emotion, not an expression of personality but an escape from personality'—a point to which he returns again and again. In great poetry there is always a distinction between the man 'who suffers and the mind which creates'. Even Shakespeare, the soul of impersonality and 'negative capability', was constantly struggling to transmute his personal agonies into the stuff of universal art. The advance of the poet in artistic maturity is always to be measured by the degree of his success to generalize and depersonalize his personal emotions and experiences which are generally his starting point:

> The abstract conception
> Of private experience at its greatest intensity,
> Becoming universal which we call poetry,
> May be affirmed in verse.

One way of achieving this release from personal bias and private emotions is the adoption of a dramatic technique of expression, described in his famous phrase, 'objective correlative'—'a set of objects, a situation, a chain of events which shall be the formula of that particular emotion'. Artistic creation, which is an attempt to organize the chaotic feelings and images into a pattern, is, in itself, an effective way of mastering, controlling and depersonalizing the 'squads of personal emotions'. Impersonality is achieved, further, through the individual artist's allegiance to some authority outside himself, which Eliot regarded as the hall-mark of the 'classic'. This external authority, in his early writings, is literary and cultural which takes the whole of Europe as a single unit and English literature itself as an integral part of the entire literature of the West from the time of Homer to this day. The point, is discussed at length in his oft-quoted essay, *Tradition and the Individual Talent'*, which wisely reconciles the claims of convention with, the necessity of individual freedom and new experiments. Allegiance to tradition rests upon historical consciousness, the awareness not only 'of the pastness of the past, but also of its presence'. Eliot is at pains to emphasize the dynamic nature of tradition which is in a process of constant modification by the advent of literary masterpieces in the later epochs. A great work of to-day automatically alters the existing order in literature and, likewise, even the most original artist of the modern age may, in fact, be under the greatest obligation to the old masters of art and poetry Thus the words of the dead are 'tongued with fire', but every fresh generation has to translate them into its own idiom. In his later writings, however, tradition becomes more and more precisely identified with the Christian dogma and the Christian way of life where the individual is subordinated to the authority of the Church and is content to live as an active member of a community where internal conflicts and tensions are not detrimental to its unity and solidarity in essential matters.

Side by side with this development, Eliot manifestly shifts his ground from poetry as an autonomous discipline to poetry as criticism of society, from an insistent need to separate poetry and religion to the paramount necessity of uniting the two for mutual enrichment and the redemption of the contemporary society from the slough of secularism. It is not without significance that the spiritual ordering of experience in his *Four Quartets* clearly invokes the analogy of the artistic pattern in the verbal structure of poetry, and in his *Poetry and Drama* the function of art is described in terms of spiritual and mystic repose:

> ....it is ultimately the function of art, in imposing a credible order upon ordinary reality, and thereby eliciting some perception of order in reality to bring us to a condition of serenity, stillness and reconciliation.

Eliot has insisted upon the maturity of classicism as distinguished from the immaturity of the romantic art and temper. Part of this maturity lies in what he describes as 'unified sensibility', the unity of thought and feeling, the capacity to present 'emotional equivalents of thought', which means that poetry is not a 'spontaneous overflow of powerful feelings', but the art of making emotion capable of intellectual formulation. The mature art is an amalgamation of 'disparate experiences', of gravity with levity, of the sordid with the sublime; here 'intellect is at the tip of the senses and senses are the channels of thought. Poetry is not inspiration but organization and the poetic mind is the creative crucible where thoughts, sensations, images and experiences are constantly forming new wholes. One recalls a striking statement in his essay, *The Metaphysical Poets:*

> "When a poet's mind is perfectly equipped for its work, it is constantly amalgamating disparate experiences; the ordinary man's experience is chaotic, irregular, fragmentary. The latter falls in love, or reads Spinoza and these two experiences have nothing to do with each other, or with the noise of the typewriter or the smell of cooking; in the mind of the poet these experiences are always making new wholes."

The unified sensibility also implies the need of combining the creative and the critical operations of the mind. Eliot is at pains to stress the supreme necessity for the poet to follow the ideal of Horace, to write in a heat and correct at leisure, or the practice of Virgil who brought forth his verses like the young ones of a she-wolf (uncouth and misshapen at birth) and licked them into shape later on.

> "The larger part of the labour of an author is critical: the labour of sifting, combining, constructing, expunging, correcting, testing." (Selected Essays—p. 30)

He agreed with the Romantics that the poet is a maker or creator like God himself, but he was, at the same time, acutely aware of the fundamental difference between the two processes of creation, divine and human. God's omnipotence had only to wish to bring about His creation—God said there should be light and there was light. But the human creator, with his limited capacity and shabby tools, has to struggle hard and painfully to raise his verbal fabric of 'dainty devices'. Robert Bridges has put the essence of this labour and pain in the mouth of the nightingale, the type of all singers, to enforce the strain and struggle behind the song:

> a throe of the heart
> Whose pining visions dim, forbidden hopes profound
> No dying cadence nor long sigh can sound for all our art.

Eliot's pronouncement on this point is equally emphatic and poignant:

> Out of the meaningless practical shapes of all that is living or lifeless
> Joined with the artist's eye, new life, new form, new colour.
> Out of the sea of sound, the life of music,
> Out of the slimy mud of words, out of the sleet and hail of verbal imprecisions,
> Approximate thoughts and feelings, words that have taken the place of thoughts and feelings,
> There spring the perfect order of speech, and the beauty of incantation.
> The work of creation is never without travail.

The classical ideal of poetic expression and function is concentrated in Pope's dictum: 'What oft was thought but never so well expressed', and Eliot's remarks reflect his full concurrence. He has reminded us, not infrequently, that even the greatest poets, like Dante and Shakespeare, may have to depend upon a given stock of thoughts and beliefs, which they should have the skill and capacity to enliven and vitalise by the magic of their language. Unfortunately language, the chief instrument of the poet, is 'a shabby equipment always deteriorating' and Eliot's awareness of this fact is as poignant as that of Horace in *Ars Poetica.* We recall the well-known passage:

> Words strain.
> Crack and sometimes break, under the burden,
> Under the tension, slip, slide, perish,
> Decay with imprecision, will not stay in place,
> Will not stay still.

The poet takes this social instrument and endeavours to arrest its tendency towards deterioration and ossification under the pressure, so great to-day, of science, commerce and journalism. It is the imaginative handling of the instrument by poetic artists which keeps it alive and mobile, fit for digesting new objects, new thoughts and new feelings, as he aptly observes in his essay on the poetry of Swinburne. The poet should be eminently possessed of what Eliot has described, rather ambiguously, as 'auditory imagination':

> ....the feeling for syllable and rhythm, penetrating far below the conscious levels of thought and feeling, invigorating every word; sinking to the most primitive and forgotten, returning to the origin and bringing something back, seeking the beginning and the end. It works through meanings certainly, or not without meanings in the ordinary sense, and fuses the old and the obliterated and the trite, the current and the new and surprising, the most ancient and the most civilized mentality.' *(Use of Poetry and Use of Criticism).*

The passage reminds us that Eliot belonged to the generation of Joyce and the late symbolists with Flaubert and Pater in the background. He is more than alive to the immense potentialities of single words and words in combination and the aura of association which they may acquire from their contexts elsewhere. He lived in habitual and loving commerce with the masters of the potent word, and has described, with approval and admiration, the astonishing skill of Lancelot Andrewes, one of his favourite authors: 'Andrewes takes a word and derives the World from it; squeezing and squeezing the word until it yields the full juice of meaning which we should never have supposed any word to possess'. This is what Eliot himself has done in his mature poetry.

But the handling of language by the poets also is not free from danger. In course of time it may become too poetical, formal and stereotyped, too remote from the living language of the people. From time to time, therefore, it is necessary that attempt should be made to infuse new life and vitality into the dull and formal diction by bringing the poetic language into the living contact with the current speech. This is an old truth dating back to Aristotle, Longinus and Horace and the reactions of Donne, Jonson and Wordsworth, author of the Preface to the *Lyrical Ballads* (1800), are only the popularly known illustrations of it. Eliot was convinced, with his contemporary compeers, that language, like Antaeus, sucks fresh life and energy from the soil in which it should be rooted. Like Horace he presents his ideal of composition or verbal organization in the following oft-quoted lines:

> ....where every word is at home
> Taking its place to support the others,
> The word neither diffident nor ostentatious,
> An easy commerce of the old and the new,
> The common word exact without vulgarity,
> The formal word precise but not pedantic,
> The complete consort dancing together.

The architects of the modernist poetry were rightly convinced that poetic language had become exhausted, imprecise and disjointed through the peculiar handling of the Romantics and their Victorian followers. The crying need of the hour was the fashioning of a new instrument to meet the demands of a complex age; the old verse-forms and rhythmic structures seemed too hackneyed and static to register the confusion, complexity and contradictions inherent in the sensibilities of a scientific and industrialized society. Robert Bridges, the veteran technician of the verse craft in the later Victorian age, had already voiced the need for verse-reform:

> 'In all art when a great master appears he so exhausts the material at his disposal as to make it impossible for any succeeding artist to be original, unless he can find either some new material or invent some new method of handling the old.............there are abundant signs that English syllabic verse has long been in the state of artistic exhaustion of form which follows great artistic efforts.'

The remark lends support to Eliot's conviction that Shakespeare has made a blank-verse tragedy impossible to-day, just as Milton has done the blank verse epic.

Eliot has defined the aim of the makers of modern poetry in not a few of his critical pronouncements which illustrate his own practice:

> "It was one of our tenets that verse should have the virtue of prose, diction should become assimilated to cultivated contemporary speech, before aspiring to the elevation of Poetry............Subject-matter and imagery of poetry should be extended to topics and objects related to the modern life. We were to seek the non-poetic, to seek even material refractory to transmutation into poetry, and words and phrases which had not been used in poetry before."

His own preferences and prejudices concerning the poets and writers, old and new, were determined by these tenets. His starting point was the conviction that the English poetry, by the first decade of the 20th century, had become feeble and insular and must be revitalized through its contact with the continental literature:

> 'I do not think it is too sweeping to say that there was no poet, in England and America, who could have been of use to a beginner in 1908. The only recourse was to poetry of another age and of another language',

He was to write in *Poetry,* September, 1946, it was necessary that English poetry of the day should be 'crossed' by more vital poetry of the continent, just as the poetic diction was to be 'crossed' by prose idiom and speech-rhythm; and the widening of the English mental horizon, similarly, required a more fruitful alertness about the larger European tradition:

> "The struggle of our time is to re-establish a vital connection between the individual and the race...........

to make the poet aware of ' the mind' of Europe, the accumulated wisdom of time."

The continental literature which Eliot proposed to adopt as the instrument of this regeneration and rejuvenation was the French literature of the late 19th century which was dominated by the symbolists. He lighted upon Symons' seminal book, *The Symbolist Movement in Literature* (1899) which opened his eyes to a new poetry and new technique which seemed to answer the necds of the young intellectual, preparing for his poetic venture. At a later date he frankly acknowledged his debt to several figures of the movement, Baudelaire, Carbiere and Laforgue:

> "From Baudelaire I learnt the poetical possibilities of the more sordid aspects of the modern metropolis, of the possibility of fusion between the sordidly realistic and the phantasmagoric, the possibility of juxtaposition of the matter-of-fact and the fantastic and that the source of new poetry might be found in what had been regarded as the impossible, the sterile, the intractable, unpoetic."
>
> (*Adelphi, 1951*).

Laforgue attracted him by similar qualities, because he also, like Corbiere before him, had tried to get rid of all worn-out poetic words, to forge language to express new feelings of urban civilization and work out a sort of poetic shorthand, to register the working of a mind simultaneously possessed of diverse and conflicting feelings. His art combined great freedom and flexibility of versification with precise and vivid images drawn from sources grand as well as prosaic. The symbolic technique, in general, may be briefly characterized, in the words of Wilson, as a medley of images, deliberately mixed metaphors, the combination of the grand and the prosaic manners, the bold amalgamation of the material with the spiritual.

This interest in the French symbolists must have confirmed Eliot's preference for the English Metaphysical poets, especially Donne and Marvell, and the Jacobean dramatists who lived in a world of chaos and anxiety similar to our own, standing neck-deep amid the wrecks of the old orderly universe gone to pieces under the impact of new ideas and outlook of life, striving as best they could to 'shore the fragments against their ruin' and contrive some order, however momentary and precarious, out of the 'heap of broken images'. They also had reacted against the stereotyped diction, imagery and sentiments of the Sonneteers and the elaborate opulence and highly stylized manner of Spenser, to cultivate a familiar and colloquial style, a complex and flexible rhythm and an intricate and all-inclusive texture of poetry, descending to materials grossly commonplace, grotesque and non-poetical and soaring up into the realms of the sublime and spiritually noble and thrilling:

> "What Donne strove to devise was a medium of expression", says Eliot, "that would correspond to the felt intimacy of his existence, that would suggest sudden contrasts, by harsh dissonance as well as by harmonies, the actual sensation of life as he himself had experienced it.........the conversational tone, the vocabulary at once colloquial and surprisingly strange, rapid association of ideas, irregular verse and difficult sentence-structure as a part of fidelity to thought and feeling, the flash of wit resulting from the shock of contrasts".

The remark, one may assert, gives a fair outline of Eliot's own programme of poetic reform, which he in turn recommended to his felow cultivators of the new poetry, calculated to record the artist's awareness of the complex modern consciousness:

> "It appears likely", he observes in the context of the true bearing of the Metaphysical manner upon the contemporary poetic technique, "the poets in our civilization, as it exists at present, must be difficult. Our civilization comprehends great variety and complexity, and this variety and complexity playing upon a refined sensibility, must produce various and complex results. The poet must become more and more comprehensive, more allusive, more indirect, doing violence to the syntax, in order to force, to dislocate, if nesessary, language into his meaning".
>
> (*Selected Essays*, p. 289)

It followed as a corollary that the formal iambic measure so long dominant must be broken and made flexible and even malleable to accommodate the changing tempo of the modern mind and the clash and interplay of opposite thoughts and feelings. The jarring discords and grating sounds and noises so characteristic of the modern way of life cannot be expressed in the mellifluous verse of a Tennyson or the monotonous though complex and obstreperous harmonies of a Swinburne. Eliot, however, was not in full sympathy with the free verse movement currently fashionable in France and, to a lesser extent, in England. His rejection is clear and emphatic, as is borne out by his article, '*Reflections on Vers Libre* (*The New Statesman*, March, 1917):

'*Vers libre* does not exist—it is a battle cry of freedom and there is no freedom in art'. He was convinced that 'even in the freest of the Free verse there should lurk the ghost of some simple metre which should advance menacingly as we doze and withdraw as we arouse'. He naturally approved the more cautious experiment of Laforgue:

> "The *Verse libre of* Jules Laforgue is free verse in much the way that the later verse of Shakespeare, Webster, and Tourneur is free verse : that is to say, it stretches, contracts and distorts the traditional French measure as later Elizabethan and Jacobean poetry......the blank verse measure."

Eliot himself followed this process and achieved an extra-ordinarily flexible and multi-toned verse responsive to the varying demands of his complex lyrical, dramatic, satirical, devotional and philosophically and religiously contemplative moods and emotions.

Eliot has admitted, what his poetry fully confirms, that Dante has remained throughout the most significant single influence on his poetry. The grand representative of mediaeval Catholicism, at once most personal and most traditional, narrowly dogmatic and essentially European, the explorer of Inferno who, at last, climbed to Paradise, through suffering and contrition, with a manner highly economical, precise and pictorial, but also complex and profound, an uncompromising rebel, corrosive in his hatred and animosity, yet imbued with the patriotic zeal to refine the 'dialect of the tribe' and exalt his native language through hard and painful effort, Dante was best fitted to strike many and most intimate chords in the heart of Eliot who was launching upon a similar but more difficult poetic mission in an age given wholly and unreservedly to secular concerns.

It is, indeed, impossible to enumerate all the influences which were operative on a mind at once widely erudite and profoundly philosophical; yet, in passing, we may refer to his keen interest in Greek tragedy and mythology, (as interpreted by the Anthropologists of the day) evident in his plays and many of his poems, and, among his contemporary writers, single out Joyce and American Henry James, and Ezra Pound for special mention. His favourite modern philosopher was Bradley, whose *Appearance and Reality* practically charts out his mental progress from early cynicism to later mysticism, though his spiritual exploration is presented in Christian terms and his debt to Augustine, St. John of the Cross and other mediaeval mystics is self-evident. Among ancient philosophers, Aristotle and Plato are generally at the back of many of his ideas and the Heraclitean philosophy of flux and creative tension of opposites precariously reconciled colours many of his meditative passages in the *Four Quartets.* He was attracted to Buddhism with its emphasis upon the ubiquity of pain and suffering in human life, swayed by desires and sensuous appetites, and the necessity of renunciation and ascetic discipline for real peace and emancipation of the mind and the soul. The wisdom of Hindu philosophy and mysticism was quite congenial to his peculiar temper and the cult of 'detached action' preached by Lord Krishna in *Bhagavad Gītā* proved especially helpful to his point of view. The theme of Time, mechanical as well as psychological, which becomes so prominent in his later poetry, clearly testifies to his indebtedness to Bergsonian Theory of *duree*, that the present is a living centre of past and future and time as a continuum cannot be split up into mutually exclusive units:

> Time present and time past
> Are both perhaps present in time future,
> And time future contained in time past.
>
> ....
>
> What might have been and what has been
> Point to one end, which is always present.

It is time now to stop this cataloguing of influences which can never exhaust the innumerable constituents of a mind widely informative and extraordinarily receptive of impressions and experiences, observations of life and contemplations of literature, which were constantly blending together to form new wholes—a process which Coleridge, among others, has described as one of reducing heterogeneity into unity, the many into one, as the hallmark of the plastic imagination. It will need a scholarly labourer more perceptive, patient and encyclopaedic than even the celebrated author of *The Road to Xanadu* to do full justice to this 20th century incarnation of the polyglot 'logician, metaphysician and bard' of Lamb's lyrical invocation.

ELIOT'S POETIC PILGRIMAGE

We now pass from Eliot's critical ideals to his poetic reality, which shows a clear and logical evolution from the beginning to the end of his career. There is one basic idea which determines the direction of his development and prompts the changes in his style, diction, imagery and technique. The principle may best be described in his own words: 'The whole of the modern life is corrupted by what I call secularism, that is simply unaware simply cannot understand the meaning of, the primacy of the supernatural over the natural life, of something I assume to be our primary concern." It is this religious bias which runs as a unifying thread through his works and gives them a remarkable consistency. The early poems reflect this point of view negatively while the later poetry marks the change to the positive aspect of it. In the former the secular society occupies the centre and its superficial glamours, but spiritual emptiness are exposed with an ironical detachment and corrosive scrutiny which border on cynicism. But all the while the spiritual and moral values of the past, embodied in myths and in the teachings of Christ and his Apostles, are constantly present in the background, and are, at times, even harshly juxtaposed with the lack of all values in contemporary life as a measure of the depth of confusion and anarchy prevalent in our age of anxiety. But as Eliot advances towards his later and more personal poetry, he manages to shift the centre of his vision from history in time to the timeless realities of the spirit. The world of low dreams is crossed with the realm of the high vision, and natural life is given meaning and significance in terms of the higher supernatural order to which it is clearly linked. It is a passage from 'appearance' to 'reality', from the kingdom of death to the sphere of light and life, from Dante's Hell to his Purgatory, with a momentary glimpse of the Paradise above it. It is an enactment of the theme of death and rebirth and may not inaptly be compared to the progress of Shakespeare from the depth of the tragic period to the height, however uncertain, in his last plays. Critics of Shakespeare have noted the change which comes over his style, imagery and symbolism in the later plays, how the images of darkness, disease and decomposition of things peculiar to the tragic period yield place to those drawn from the beauty, fertility, growth and fruitfulness of nature. The old world of evil, discord and ravenous passion is still there, but it is lighted from above by the grace of heaven which bends over it like a benediction. The old generation of strife-torn and hardened humanity finds a source of reconciliation and repose in a growing generation of young children, innocent and free from the taint of worldliness, whose very presence is a potent charm to chase evil and wickedness from the corrupt world of men. In Eliot also, the gloomy, sterile and stony wilderness of early poems gradually changes into a land of potential fertility, the bones begin to sing and the fire of lust and desire becomes purgatorial, destructive water resumes its transforming function, the song of birds is soothing to the weary spirit, which is able at last to recall the garden full of the voices of children. The curse of death recedes and the spirit is free enough to catch at least fleeting visions of the light 'whose smile kindles the universe', and of the 'still centre', the 'word within the word', round which the distracted world revolves like a whirling wheel. In a moving passage, cited in George Eliot's *Silas Marner*, if I remember well, there is a feeling reference to the early days of humanity when angels used to appear on the earth to hold the storm-tossed mortals by the hand and lead them to the heaven of security and rest. The angels now have deserted our sinful planet but their place is taken by children to redeem man from the dark prison of life which has closed round him. Shakespeare and Eliot illustrate the truth of this belief in striking ways peculiar to each of them:

> What is this face, less clear and clearer
> The pulse in the arm, less strong and stronger—
> Given or lent ? more distant than stars and nearer than
> the eye
> Whispers and small laughter between leaves and hurrying
> feet
> Under sleep, where all the waters meet.—(*Marina*-17-21)

In the early poems (1909-1920), however, the garden is quite remote and children are not yet born. We are confronted with a set of sophisticated men and women, 'refined beyond civilization', flippant, timorous and diseased, tied to the superficial monotony of a dull existence, with its recurrent round of tea-parties, frivolous amusements, low aims and sordid cares, quite oblivious of the meaning of old values, cultural, moral and religious. The poems are in the nature of dramatic lyrics, expressing the mental operations of the *dramatis personae*, created by the poet to represent the social group he had the occasion to observe and study at close quarters. Williamson has rightly observed:

> "His lyric themes are generally complex, requiring complicated procedures. They are often dramatic in nature, employing the impersonal projection, but treating not so much of conflict in action as in thought and emotion, where antithesis, paradox, incompatible metaphor, irony and other forms of discord or discordant concord become the proper means of expression. Often the expression depends on the association, not resemblance, of ideas".

Eliot is using, in short, 'interior monologue,' the psychological version of Browning's dramatic monologue, with its root in the sub-conscious mind of the character, who is just exhaling the confused medley of memories and desires lying in some obscure depth of the consciousness, with a connection which is not easily amenable to the laws of logic, but is clearly the product of what the psychologists have described as 'mental jumps'. Dujardin, one of the earliest exponents of this form, has defined it as a speech of a given character, designed to introduce us directly into the internal life of this character, without the character's intervening; a discourse without listener and unspoken. Here we have the most intimate thoughts closest to the unconsciousness, no logical organization but a faithful record of the processes of thought in its original state and as it comes into the mind. Even direct sentences may be reduced to their syntactical minimum and an air of formlessness deliberately achieved.

The landscape is in perfect accord with the thoughts of the character because the external setting is simply a reflection of the psychological state. This 'psychological landscape' was fully warranted by the contemporary art and philosophy and Bradley had defined 'appearance' in terms of the complete subjectivity of perception, a merger of the object in the subject, a re-creation of the external nature in the light of the pre-occupation of the mind, which is fitly illustrated by Coleridge in *Dejection, an Ode*.

We have to analyse a few of these poems in order to understand the mysteries of Eliot's manner and technique. *The Love Song of J. Alfred Pruforck* (1917) is the most representative poem of the early group and a fair sample of Eliot's characteristic diction, versification and technique in general. The character is a representative of the cultured Boston society, intimately known to the poet and his name, 'Prufrock' is quite symptomatic of the shy, timid, unmanly nature of the speaker as he himself later describes it:

> Politic, cautious and meticulous,
> Full of high sentence, but a bit obtuse
> At times, indeed, almost ridiculous—
> Almost, at times, the Fool.

The point is underlined in the epigraph from Dante's *Inferno* where a timid soul, with an overwhelming sense of fear for public opinion, is unlocking his heart to the poet under the impression that he also is the denizen of the kingdom of the dead from 'whose bourne no traveller ever returned to the earth.' "If I thought my answer were to one who ever should return to the world, this flame should shake no more". So the poem is not a dialogue between two persons 'you and I', but an internal debate between two sides of the speaker's own mind, what he is and what he would be.

> Let us go then you and I,
> When the evening is spread out against the sky
> Like a patient etherised upon a table,

We notice here the colloquial style and an original image, unpoetical but quite striking in its modernity and its symbolic significance. It is an objectification of the speaker's own personality, 'like a mind under ether conscious, but conscious of nothing'. Same is the case with other details of the setting :

> Streets that follow like a tedious argument of insidious intent

where the startling comparison cannot obscure the serious intention of the poet, which is to present the mental stalemate of the speaker. Then, while in the room the women come and go 'talking of Michaelangelo', and the glory of the Renaissance art, the fog is settling upon the scene to enforce the sordidness of their actual life :

> The yellow fog that rubs its back upon the window-panes
> The yellow smoke that rubs its muzzle on the window-panes
> Licked its tongue into the corners, of the evening,
> Lingered upon the pools that stand in drains—etc.

The description chimes in with the nature of the speaker to nicety. In the following lines the speaker makes a rapid survey of his social life with perhaps an unconscious irony:

> There will be time, there will be time
> To prepare a face to meet the faces that you meet
> And time for the works of days of hands
> That lift and drop a question on your plate :
> Time for you and time for me.
> And time yet for a hundred indecisions,
> And for a hundred visions and revisions,
> Before the taking of a toast and tea.

We notice here the remarkable economy of art in the description of the speaker's nature and way of life; we notice also the sly allusiveness, the understatement and the use of bathos or anti-climax. Thus, 'works and days' remind us of Hesiod's famous poem which celebrates the hard life of the farmer, but here the whole labour leads to the 'dropping of a question on your plate', i.e. an intensification of indecision. The words flash back to the story of John, the Baptist, whose head was brought on a platter at the instance of Herod. From this height we abruptly descend to 'toast and tea'. The essence of the matter lies in the straight question: I wonder, 'Do I dare?' and, 'Do I dare ?' and the ironical answer is provided by the words that follow:

> Time to turn back and descend the stair,
> With a bald spot in the middle of my hair—

Nothing can describe the cowardice of the man more simply but scathingly. Then after glancing at the daily routine of tea-parties powerfully condensed in the apparently trivial, but actually intense image—'I have measured out my life with coffee-spoons', the speaker introduces one of the key words in Eliot's poetry, 'the eyes':

> The eyes that fix you in a formulated phrase,
> And when I am formulated, sprawling on a pin,
> When I am pinned and wriggling on the wall.

The speaker has become a helpless worm on the point of a needle, wriggling in vain for release. This is indecision and cowardice in matters of sex, before eyes, attractive but mercilessly searching, which make his desire cold:

> Then how should I begin
> To spit out all the but-ends of my days and ways ?

His life is almost like a smoked cigar with useless fragments lingering in his memory. He can remember only the 'arms that are braceleted and white and bare' and the 'perfume from the dress' which remind him only of his indecision:

> And should I then presume ?
> And how should I begin ?

Out of sheer disgust at his indecision he envies the lot of sea-creatures which suddenly catch their prey and disappear:

> I should have been a pair of ragged claws
> Scuttling across the floors of silent seas.

The self-weariness is deepened by the image of evening, sleeping peacefully 'smoothed by long fingers, asleep, tired' etc. The self-analysis is resumed with a disclaimer that he is not a bold martyr like John, the Baptist, because his moment of greatness flickers before the prospect of Death, the 'eternal Footman'. He glances at what 'might have been', a resolute grasping of the universe in a positive hour, a determined unlocking of his heart, like Lazarus, risen from the grave and willing to share his experiences with others. The deflation comes with 'No ! I am not Prince Hamlet'. He may be living in a prison and canvassing the problem—to be or not to be—hesitating and procrastinating like the Prince of Denmark, noted for his tragic intensity, but he is cut out for the part of old Polonius, the politic Fool. But he has had the vision of beautful life, lived in a vital connection with the elements—a vision of 'mermaids singing to each other' The vision of primal beauty rises for a moment from the depth of his sub-conscious, 'the chambers of the sea' in a fit of dream which, however, is suddenly lost under the clanking of the tea cups and chatter of the human imbeciles around him:

> Till human voices wake us and we drown.

The abrupt contrast between 'waking' and 'drowning' collocated in one context is a characteristic of Eliot's technique.

We may now briefly review only the significant extracts from a few, at least, of the poems of this early group in order to illuminate the ideas and the technique which characterize and define them. *Portrait of a Lady* introduces another divided soul of this society of brittle and superficial refinement where the communication between one heart and another is well-nigh impossible:

'Yet with these April sun-sets, that somehow recall
My buried life, and Paris in the spring,
I feel immeasurably at peace, and find the world
To be wonderful and youthful, after all',

This memory only seems to exacerbate her disgust of the social routine in her fashionable life:

I shall sit here, serving tea to friends
And I must borrow every changing shape
To find expression......dance, dance
Like a dancing bear,
Cry like a parrot, chatter like an ape.

A sordid life, indeed, when a man or woman dances to the tunes of external decorum.

Preludes is another meditation upon this meaningless existence:

I am moved by fancies that are curled
Around these images, and cling,
The notion of some infinitely gentle
Infinitely suffering thing.
    Wipe your hand across your mouth, and laugh;
The worlds revolve like ancient women
Gathering fuel in vacant lots.

Another picture of this fruitless 'mental motion and gyration' comes in *Rhapsody on a Windy Night:*

Midnight shakes the memory
As a mad man shakes a dead geranium.

But this shaking throws up only lifeless wrecks:

The memory throws up high and dry
A crowd of twisted things;
A twisted branch upon the beach
Eaten smooth, and polished
As if the world gave up
The secret of its skeleton.

This is the picture of a society which has completely divorced itself from the primary springs of life and one watches only a set of moving puppets, mere gestures and grimaces, as the bond of sympathy between man and man is broken and life has lost its purpose:

> I am aware of the damp souls of housemaids;
> Sprouting despondently at area gates.

Even those who are moving about are by no means less mechanical and lifeless:

> The brown waves of fog toss up to me
> Twisted faces from the bottom of the street,
> And tear from a passer-by with muddy skirts
> And aimless smile that hovers in the air,
> And vanishes along the level of the roofs.

This brings us to the most powerful poem of the group, *Mr. Appollinax*, where a figure of almost savage vitality is brought into a shattering opposition to the world of Mr. Prufrock. Appollinax (modelled, they say, on Bertrand Russell, the English philosopher and mathematician) is a compound of Apollo and the Devil and breaks like a lusty bull into the China-shop of the over-refined and routine-ridden society the poet has been dissecting:

> His laughter tinkled among the tea cups,

and he appeared to be one of the pagan gods of natural fertility and primal energy:

> I thought of Fragilian, that shy figure among the beech trees,
> And Priapus in the shrubbery
> Gaping at the lady in the swing.

This animal vitality makes the fashionable apes around him, Mrs. Phalaccus and Professor Channing—Cheetah, only painted dragons. Appollinax is the embodiment of that hidden submarine life of whieh Mr. Prufrock can have only a momentary glimpse:

> He laughed like an irresponsible foetus.
> His laughter was submarine and profound
> Like the old man of the sea's
> Hidden under coral islands.

The crowning image for this vital creature is the Centaur, half human and half animal, strength of mind and compelling physical energy rolled in one:

> I heard the b*eat* of Centaur's hoofs over the hard turf,
> As his dry and passionate talk devoured the afternoon.

It is only after his departure that his overawed hosts begin to wag their petty tongues:
"There was something he sald that I might have challenged.' Of this the quiet comment of the observer is a withering condemnation:

> I remember a slice of lemon, and a bitten macaroon.

The last poem, *La Figlia Che Piange,* closes with the picture of a love-lorn lady, a counterpart of the Hyacinth-girl in *The Waste Land:*

> 'She turned away, but with the Autumn Weather
> Compelled by imagination many days,
> Many days and many hours :
> Her hair over her arms and her arm full of flowers'.

In the second group of Poems (1920) the area of the poet's observation is widened and his technique becomes more complex. It is now the whole of the modern civilization which is etched trenchantly against the permanent framework of myth and religion, a definite emergence of Eliot's mythical method which reaches its apex in *The Waste Land.*

The key-note is struck in the complex poem, *Gerontion* (1920) which is a devastating but concentrated criticism of our modern soulless civilization, which Eliot has pictured at greater length in *The Waste Land.* In an illuminating article, under the caption of *Gerontion and the Meaning of History,* in P.M.L.A., Vol. 73, 1958, Mr. Hervey Gross has shown, quite convincingly, that the poem is a meditation upon the meaningless flux of history, whose neck was broken by the irruption of new forces let loose by the Renaissance which concentrated upon the potentialities of man in isolation from his spiritual fountain-head. History has become a cheat and may be visualized as a 'devastating, indefinable, almost mystical force, driving Europe towards cultural dissolution and moral despair,' with an irresistible, shattering and crippling energy. Eliot's indebtedness to Henry Adams, author of *Education,* is quite evident here.

In the brief analysis which follows I have drawn upon the illuminating comments occurring in *Modern Poetry,* prepared under the general editorship of Maynard Mack, Yale University, 1950. Gerontion, which means 'little old man', symbolises the twentieth century Western civilization, thoroughly depleted and despiritualized, with only faint and disturbing but ineffectual memories of its heroic, cultural and religious past lingering in its mind. The epigraph 'Thou hast nor youth nor age etc.' is taken from Shakespeare's *Measure for Measure,* which dwells upon the vanity of earthly life and, in these lines, sets the pace for the dream-like movement of the speaker's mind, who describes himself in the feeling words of A. C. Benson in the life of Edward Fitzgerald:

> Here I am, an old man in a dry month,
> Being read to by a boy, waiting for rain.

Drought and rain are the key-symbols in *The Waste Land* also for spiritual barrenness and spiritual fertility respectively. The mind of the old man wanders back to the heroic past which contrasts sharply with the impotent present. 'I was neither at the hot gates etc.' refers to the heroism of the Greeks at Thermopylae and the dauntless courage of Elizabethan explorers braving great dangers in the foreign, inhospitable countries. He returns to his present condition, 'My house is a decayed house', and its sordid surroundings. The house-owner is a jew, as the contemporary Europe was actually ruled and exploited by the Jewish merchants and money-lenders. The beastliness of the Jew is powerfully conveyed by the highly significant words used in his description. He was *spawned* in Antwerp, *blistered* in Brussels and *patched and peeled* in London. The picture of decay is completed by the coughing goat, *'rocks, moss, stone crop, iron, merds,* the dead limbs of our industrial civilization, and by the kitchen woman who sneezes at evening, poking the peevish gutter.' The landscape, of course, is mental and psychological, the posturings of an old man's 'dull head among windy spaces.'

With the passage *Signs are taken for Wonders* we are introduced to the Christian idea of Incarnation, the Son of God, lying in a trough, the reference being clearly to Lancelot Andrewes' 'Nativity Sermon.' The preacher dwells upon the great mystery of the divine Babe, *Word Within a Word*, symbol of Logos, source of all knowledge, wisdom and speech, but lying as a 'dumb child unable to speak a word'; the source of all light but 'swaddled with darkness', the divine omnipotence that, according to Job, 'taketh the vast body of the main sea, turns it to and fro and rolls it about with the swaddling bands of darkness' shown here as a helpless child wrapped in cloth and confined in the dark tub. This is the great wonder but the blind men of today are unable to see or understand it and cry aloud, 'we would see a sign', like the foolish Scribes and Pharisees in the Bible who were rebuked by Christ: 'an evil and adulterous generation seeketh after a sign; and there shall no sign be given to it'. The remark unites the present-day humanity to that generation in the past. 'In the juvenescence of the year came Christ the tiger' is a remarkable instance of Eliot's compressed, allusive and indirect technique of expression. He takes the phrase 'Christ, a wild cat' from Andrewes' sermon and associates it with the mystery of Blake's 'Tiger, burning bright,' a symbol of God's strength and savage energy. Then Christ is associated with the fertility gods who were killed and devoured by their worshippers, as Christ is done by Christians, to indicate that man's health and vitality depends upon his capacity to absorb the power and energy of God into himself. But the juvenescence of the year, the spring season, is also the sixteenth-century Renaissance in European history when Christ and his energy came to be ignored by the exponents of the new movement, described here in terms of the spring vegetation—'In *depraved* May, *dogwood* and chestnut, flowering *judas* etc., where the three key words, 'depraved', 'dogwood' and 'judas' glance at the passionate animal energy of the new civilization which was a betrayal of Christ—a new Judas, who sold away Christ for thirty silver coins. This new generation was not capable of killing and eating its God, symbol of spiritual fertility, for its strength. It had grown so feeble spiritually that it destroyed its God 'among whispers'. The catalogue of names that follows introduces us to the dregs of this secular civilization, who have lost their roots in the swamp of internationalism, grown lately fashionable in the commercial culture or lack of culture in Europe.

'Vacant shuttles weave the wind' is the most cutting criticism of the vacancy and utter futility of the life of these people, physical as well as mental. The speaker has no 'ghosts' because his present is cut off from the significant past, and modern history, isolated from the divine Logos, has become barren of meaning, a deceitful elf, whose lesson is either meaningless or it comes at a time when we are mentally distracted and unprepared:

> ......And what she gives, gives with such supple
> Confusions that the giving famishes the craving
> Gives too late what's not believed in.

Under such circumstances values have become transposed and 'virtue' and 'vice' have lost their distinction, so that a human criminal is hailed as the hero and the soviour of a nation:

> Unnatural vices
> Are fathered by our heroism. Virtues
> Are forced upon us by our impudent crimes.

'These tears are shaken from the wrath-bearing tree', that is, the tree of the knowledge of good and evil, and also the Cross on which Christ died to purchase human salvation, both of which call for our repentance, the necessity of Passion.

The 'tiger which springs in the new year', is the irrational force of secular history, not the terrible energy of the Saviour: it does not save but destroys. In the Renaissance, however, society was capable of passionate lusts and crimes, as is implied in the remark of the voluptuous heroine in Middleton's *Changeling*'—'I that was near your heart' etc. But in the decayed society of to-day the heart itself has frozen:

'I have lost my passion......I have lost my sight' etc. So these memories of the impotent speaker only 'excite the membrane, when the sense has cooled'. The old man requires artificial aids to stir up his sex-instinct, content with contemplation only of what strong men and women actually enact. He is like the lustful sovereign in Seneca who-surrounded himself in old age 'with mirrors to multiply his sexual feats and vices' of youth to titillate his dull senses.

> After such knowledge what forgiveness ?

The giving of history can bring no forgiveness because it is the contemplation of human vanities and crimes. Forgiveness is the result of love and a world torn by hate and conflict is incapable of producing it. In the closing lines the destructive self-analysis has reached the point of delirium; —he has been weaving cob-webs of thoughts like a spider. In this delirium the persons around him have lost their solidity and become mere chimeras blown up in air beyond the 'shuddering Bear' in 'fractured atoms' or whirled by the wind like 'white feather' through the parts of the sea. Here is the picture of a civilization given over to Jews and commercial potentates— 'thoughts of a dry brain in a dry season'.

Significant also is the briefer but equally allusive poem, *Sweeney Among the Nightingales,* where, for the first time, Eliot views the squalid world of to-day against the mythical background to bring the meaninglessness of life in the contemporary society in sharp contrast with a period where life and death were equally fruitful. It is here that the myth of Philomela, so rudely forced by the barbarous king, Tereus, is given a prominence which it retains in *The Waste Land.* Philomela raped and mutilated gave herself over, heart and soul, to the purgatorial fire of suffering and was eventually transformed into the Nightingale, the bird, 'most musical and most melancholy, whose 'inviolable song' symbolizes a beauty 'made more beautiful by sorrow', which has been always there, though not properly understood by the dirty world which keeps on moving on the metalled road of appetency, leading to the blind alley of 'birth, copulation and death'.

The poem refers to two more myths, both dealing with sacrificial deaths resulting in a higher and more vigorous life. The first refers to the Greek story of Agamemnon, the leader and commander of the Greek host in the Trojan war, who was murdered by his passionate wife, Clytemnestra, on his return home from the conquest abroad. The woman in turn was murdered by her son, Orestes, in fulfilment of the god-appointed duty of avenging his murdered father. The matricide aroused the agents of Nemesis, black Furies with serpent locks, who dogged in the footsteps of the young criminal and thus plunged him into the hell of suffering and remorse. Ultimately the conflict was resolved into a higher harmony and reconciliation at Athena and the Furies were transformed into beneficent deities, the Eumenides. The story is treated in the celebrated Trilogy of Aeschylus, from which the epigraph of the poem is drawn. It is said that it was Orestes who initiated the rites of the mystery cult at Nemi, the Sacred wood of Diana, where, according to Frazer, the old king-priest was killed by the young successor who drew life and energy from his chief and victim. It was a sacrificial death which fed life and renewed youth and vitality.

This passionate and meaningful pattern is harshly juxtaposed with the world of our modern herc, Sweeney, who is at once our blind Samson, pulling the whole structure of values over his head only to be converted into a human-swine, wallowing in the mud of lust and gross materialism. He and all his companions are presented in terms of animals, fierce as will as mean and have no distinct human individualities. The epigraph refers to the cry of Agamemnon under the assassin's knife: 'O I am struck deep with a deadly blow', which may also mean that he has been killed altogether by Sweeney and his modern accomplices, representatives of a society *sans* heroism, *sans* leadership, *sans* meaningful pattern of life and death.

Sweeney is introduced as a human beast:

> Apeneck Sweeney spreads his knees
> Letting his arm hang down to laugh
> The Zebra stripes along his jaw
> Swelling to maculate giraffe.

This human-animal seems to be under the threat of murder:

> Death and the Raven drift above
> And Sweeney guards the horned gate.

The Raven is intended to remind us of the 'hoarse raven' in Shakespeare's *Macbeth*, which treats of another brutal murder which eventually led to the purgation of the corrupt society under Malcolm, symbolized as a crowned child with a green branch, a fitting herald of new birth. 'Horned gate' is not only the Homeric passage through which true intimations from the dream world used to pass to men, it may more appropriately refer to the Sacred Wood (cf. title of Eliot's first collection of Critical Essays), where the ritual death of the old priest was enacted under the emblem of the crescent moon. Thus Sweeney's sordid death receives a shattering impact from the sacrificial death in that holy place. Its sordidness is emphasized in the details that follow: Thus the drunken woman described as "the person in the Spanish cape' clashes with Sweeney only to pull the tablecloth, overturn a coffee-cup and sprawl on the floor to yawn; the 'silent man at the windowsill' *sprawls and gapes;* there is Rachel with her murderous paws, which, however, only tear at the grapes.

This brings us, in an abrupt transition, to

> The nightingales are singing near
> The convent of the Sacred heart
> And sang within the bloody wood
> When Agamemnon cried aloud, etc.

The lines are the meeting-point of Sweeney's world with that of the three myths we have described already. The nightingales 'are singing still' and 'they sang'—these phrases unite the present with the past through a needful reminder that love, lust and murder are common in every age, so is the case with the song of the nightingale, which sings indifferently to modern Sweeney as it sang at the holy death in the sacred Grove as well as above the 'dishonoured shroud of Agamemnon'. Its song, like sunlight falls alike on all, but its value can be understood only by those who are competent for the purpose. Spiritual values do not come as a gift, they are to be acquired with labour, pain and tears, through discipline and the purgation of the vision. Wordsworth lamented the fact that Nature is always overflowing with life and energy, yet men remain weak and thirst-tormented because we see nothing in Nature that is ours:

> We have given our hearts away
> A sordid boon!

With *The Waste Land* the negative first phase of Eliot's poetic progress reaches the point of culmination. In its complex and elaborate technique he has managed to combine the landscape and imagery, the searching analysis of secular history and the spider-like agility to move from one strand of thought to another, which we find in *Gerontion*, with the adoption of the mythical method, the collocation of the heroic and spiritually meaningful past with the decayed and vulgar present, strange bed-fellows, forming a concord of discord, which becomes most prominent in *Sweeney among the Nightingales*. In '*The Waste Land*' the universe of death receives the most elaborate and caustic treatment through the concentration of a multiplicity of vivid images scattered in the early poems. It is pictured of a wilderness of splintered rocks, a heap of broken images with the settled cloud of fog, the twilight atmosphere, with 'bats with baby faces crawling up and down the blackened walls', while in the air a city is breaking and dissolving, the London bridge is falling down. It is a nightmare vision through which we are made to witness the antics of the ghostly inhabitants, a crowd of benighted and empty bipeds pouring like a flock of sheep over the bridge or swarming on the arid plain, 'ringed by flat horizon only, stumbling and falling into the cracked earth. One is reminded, indeed, of the devastating and corrosive gaze of Baudelaire and the equally penetrating and lancet-keen vision which Eliot has attributed to Donne and Webster:

> Webster was much possessed by death
> And saw the skull beneath the skin;
> And breastless creatures underground
> Leaned backward with a lipless grin.
> Donne, I suppose, was such another
> Who found no substitute for sense,
> To seize and clutch and penetrate;
>   Expert beyond experience,
> He knew the anguish of the marrow
>   The ague of the skeleton;
> No contact possible to flesh
>   Allayed the fever of the bone.

We postpone further consideration of the poem to the second section of our study, where an attempt has been made to analyse its text and its technique fully and at great length.

Later Poetry:

The poems which follow *The Waste Land* mark the gradual emergence of the poet, through well-marked stages, towards a positive state of mind, the stage of reconciliation and repose, of spiritual re-birth and renewal, of the resolution of tension and harmonious union of the opposites. The course can be clearly charted out with the help of a few crucial poems which lead to the *Four Quartets*, the peak of Eliot's meditative poetry and the crowning achievement of religious consciousness in an irreligious age. The turning-point is marked by *Hollow Men*, where the landscape of *The Waste Land* is repeated but the mental outlook has definitely changed. The men are still the denizens of Dante's Limbo, wretched souls of those who lived without infamy and without fame'. Their nature is clearly reflected in their naked and stripped speech and light-footed repetitions and short-winded verse:

We are the hollow men
We are the stuffed men
    Leaning together
Headpiece filled with straw. Alas !
Our dried voices, when
We whisper together,
Are quiet and meaningless
As wind in dry grass
Or rat's feet over broken glass
    In our dry cellar;

Further reminiscences of the landscape in *The Waste Land* are quite numerous as well as striking:

    This is the dead land
    This is cactus land
    Here the stone images
    Are raised, here they receive
The supplication of a dead man's hand
Under the twinkle of a fading star.

But it will be a mistake to think that this poem is merely a simpler and briefer version of *The Waste Land.* There is a definite movement forward which distinguishes these men from the aimless humanity in the earlier poem. The hollow men are aware of their plight, which their counterparts in the earlier poem are not. In *The Waste Land* people are content with their empty life—'winter kept us warm', utterly oblivious of the fact that their low contentment is actually death:

> Those who sit in the sty of contentment, meaning
> Death
> Those who suffer the ecstasy of the animals, meaning
> Death.

The hollow men have the acute awareness, which is the first requisite of spiritual re-birth, that they are living in the kingdom of death, under the pall of darkness, and that there is the other kingdom of death and there are 'eyes' which they dare not meet but which, they believe, are the 'master-light of man's day'. In this context, therefore, the reference to Kurtz is extremely significant. His dying whisper, 'the horror' showed at least 'some sort of belief; it had candour, it had conviction, it had a vibrating note of revolt......, it had the appalling face of a glimpsed truth', the words of the hollow men almost echo the above sentiment:

> In this last of meeting places
> We grope together
> And avoid speech
> Gathered on this beach of tumid river.
> Sightless, unless

The eyes reappear
As the perpetual star
Multifoliate rose
Of death's twilight Kingdom
The hope only
    Of empty men.

They are in darkness, no doubt, but they are able to understand the meaning of the 'eyes' which once led Dante from the twilight kingdom of death to the happy regions of Paradise where he saw God's love as a vast many-petalled rose enfolding everything in its tender embrace.

In a well-argued article, *Hope for T. S. Eliot's Empty Men*, in P.M.L.A., Vol. 73, 1958, F.W. Strothmann and L. V. Ryan, have shown, quite convincingly, that in the final section of the poem the hollow men have reached the spiritual state which the mystic, John of the Cross, has described as the 'Dark Night of the Soul' free from all attachment, yet afraid to face the 'eyes' of God out of shame for the previous sin. They have reached 'the delectable desert' beyond the world of the senses which gradually dissolves without much noise:

For thine is
    Life is
For thine is the
This is the way the world ends
This is the way the world ends
This is the way the world ends
Not with a bang but a whimper.

I, for one, find no difficulty in concurring with their conclusion that the poem ends on a positive note and there is a definite promise of hope for the hollow men.

The Christian note, struck in this poem, expands and envelops the entire length and breadth of *Ash Wednesday* (1930), a complex and difficult religious poem, which marks the summit of Eliot's lyrical and devotional achievement and in the complete fusion of language, rhythm, tone and emotion into a single lyrical movement, has no parallel elsewhere in modern poetry. Here the awareness of the hollow men takes the definite Christian form of repentance and contrition and prayer and the poem is as remarkable for echoes of Liturgy as for the traditional symbols of Orthodox Christianity. The awful 'eyes' of the *Hollaw Men* are transformed into the benign eyes of the Lady, Mother and Sister, who takes the place of Belladonna, the Lady of the Rocks, in *The Waste Land,* and is a living symbol of suffering transformed into supernal beauty far superior to the 'inviolable song' of Philomela, because more human and more divine:

Lady of silences
Calm and distressed
Torn and most whole
Rose of memory
Rose of forgetfulness
Exhausted and life-giving
Worried reposeful
The single Rose
Is now the Garden
Where all loves end.
Terminate torment
Of love unsatisfied
The greater torment
Of love satisfied.

The spiritual ascent brings the conventional symbol of the three steps which lead the soul through the wistful memories of senses and their pleasures to a point where they cease to have any meaning and reality:

> Over the third stair
> Fading, fading; strength beyond hope and despair.

The turning world of senses at last acquires a meaning through its alliance with the 'unmoved mover', the God incarnate, at once in time and out of time:

> The Word without a word, the Word within
> The World and for the world;
> And the light shone in darkness and
> Against the World the unstilled world still whirled
> About the centre af the silent Word.

This is the symbol of 'the wheel and the still point' which becomes a key symbol in the *Four Quartets.* Here the opposites begin to reconcile; the Yew of death points to the Yew of the immortality, the desert blooms and fountains begin to play, birds sing and even the bones start chirping like the grass-hopper. It is a state where death and life meet and the tired soul sends out its humble prayer for release from the burden of life-in-death:

> This is the time of tension between dying and birth
> The place of solitude where three dreams cross
> Between blue rocks
> But when the voices shaken from the yew tree drift away
> Let the other yew be shaken and reply.
>
> Blessed sister, holy mother, spirit of the fountain, spirit of the garden,

Suffer us not to mock ourselves with falsehood
Teach us to care and not to care
Teach us to sit still
Even among these rocks
Our peace in His will.

More simply and clearly than in *Ash Wednesday* the theme of death and re-birth receives treatment in the earlier poem, *The Journey of the Magi*. The journey of these wise men of the East to the cradle of the newborn Saviour must be taken in a spiritual sense to signify the soul's search for a new centre of life which arises out of the dead corpse of the old one. The speaker dwells upon the hardships of the journey and the love and longing assailing them as they advanced from home to witness a birth in the foreign land. Yet, in fact, the journey only symbolizes the trial and temptations which beset the soul as it moves from the secular dispensation to the religious, and has to die in one sphere in order to be able to pass into a higher and more spiritual one. The speaker, however, has witnessed a birth which was apparently akin to his death, because his old ways of living and moving have lost all meaning to him.

We had evidence and no doubt. I had seen birth and death,
But had thought they were different; this birth was
Hard and bitter agony for us, like death, our death,
We returned to our places, these kingdoms,
But no longer at ease here, in the old dispensation
With an alien people clutching their gods.

The process is on the brink of a new birth, which is reached, in fact, in *Marina,* one of the most moving lyrics among the shorter pieces of Eliot. The new birth is symbolized by a new-born baby who is, not-mother and sister but a daughter, born of the speaker's loins and naturally stands for a fresh incarnation of his own self. Moreover, the new birth is associated with the sea, the source of all life, which in *The Waste Land*, however, is destructive and sucks the bones of the drowned Phoenician sailor into its whirlpool. But here the old ship is on the point of destruction, but there is full hope in the possibility of a new ship taking its place at once:

> This form, this face, this life
> Living to live in a world of time beyond me; let me
> Resign my life for this life, my speech for that unspoken
> The awakened, lips parted, the hope, the new ships.

The death which was 'a bitter agony' for the Magi is here a souree of ecstatic joy and the sense of liberation from the bondage of the old self is fitly symbolized by wind, sweet smell and bird song:

> Those who sharpen the tooth of the dog, meaning Death etc.
> Are become unsubstantial, reduced by a wind,
> A breath of pine. and the woodsong fog
> By this grace dissolved in place.

All these themes and images are finally gathered up and co-ordinated with greatest artistic intensity in the *Four Quartets* on a higher philosophical plane. These four poems-in-one, each in itself a symphony of five movements, are the most complex contemplative verse produced in this century and remain a unique achievement. Here poetry and music have become one and the poet has achieved an authentic voice of his own, a language transparent and absolutely free from contortion and tangled compression, yet hiding below its surface ideas and meanings difficult to be grasped by any but the initiated minds, a peculiarity which Eliot himself has noted in the poetry of Dante. Space does not permit us to undertake a detailed elucidation of these poems, which, however, all laborious and painstaking annotation and elucidation will fail to open fully to general readers, dealing, as they do, with rare mystical intuitions. We shall only examine the main themes which the poet passes under contemplation not systematically but tentatively, in a manner frankly artless and engaging, because apparently free from dogmatism. The main themes are suggested through key-symbols in a movement which is not progressive—a linear movement from one point to another—but rather circular and vertical, up and down and down and up and coming back to the starting-point but with deeper intensity.

The start is made with the epigraphs from Heraclitus, the first of which says. "Although the Word (Logos) is common to all, most men live as if they had each a private wisdom of his own", while the second refers to his theory of the reconciliation of opposites, the four elements constantly striving for the upward movement from earth to fire and down again, but 'the way up is the way down'. This is the case with individuals also who are made up of four humours, in a state of creative tension, which may move 'upward to the realm of light and warmth or downward to the realm of density, cold and dark'. Eliot relates the Heraclitean philosophy of tension and reconciliation to the wisdom and dogma of Christianity in order to transcend the flux and tension of the Greek Philosopher. Thus his Logos is transformed into Incarnation and the way-up-is-the way down concept is spiritualized through its association with the mystic process of St. John of the Cross, where the two interconnected ways refer to the spiritual ascent and descent. The flux of history is opposed to the intersection of time and eternity and the flux in the individual to a state of repose, a still point. The opposition of words to Word first refers to a release from worldly noises and distractions in the contemplation of the divine wisdom and then to the repose and balance achieved by the poetic artist in the pattern he makes of words which are a chaos of sound and meaning. The contemplation of time is at once the contemplation of racial history and personal history—the river is within and without. The river is opposed to the ocean where several voices are transcended in the clangour of the ground-swell, the tolling of the eternal bell. The first history acquires meaning when the deeper insight or understanding gained in the present enables one to see an inner order in the erstwhile flux of events and experiences. It is an attempt to unite past and present, death and life and memory and desire. The memory is the memory of childhood playing in the innocent garden in perfect tune wiih nature and also of the childhood of the race when Adam lived in Eden; and the desire is to strive to move back to that happy state from which we started as individual and as man.

The concept of the harmony of opposites is symbolized in 'dance'—dance of man and woman. the higher dance of husband and wife in the sacrament of marriage, the dance of words in poetic pattern and the higher dance where the dance ends, 'you cannot tell the dancer from the dance'. It is the detachment in action preached to Arjuna by Lord Krishna in the *Bhagavad Gītā,* the disinterested action when one is doing one's duty without any thought for its fruit, so that one is at once in the world and above it, a part of the flux, yet unaffeeted by it like a 'lotus leaf in the water—drenched yet dry,

But the deeper study is the communion of love, the love of Christ, who accepted the burden of suffering to redeem mankind and left it as a legacy to man. Suffering is the purgatorial fire in which the flames of lust and desire are consumed and the soul of the sufferer is purged of all stain. After its emergence from this ordeal, the soul realizes that what appeared to be darkness was really the shade of God's own extended hand, a token of His redeeming love, which makes even the sin of man a 'grace' in disguise and blesses the crosses of life:

Love is the unfamiliar Name
Behind the hands that wove
The intolerable shirt of flame

Which human power cannot remove.
We only live. only suspire
Consumed by either fire or fire.

We quote below the relevant passages where the above ideas are suggested or expressed. These scattered passages must be related to the discussion we have already attempted. The opening poem, *Burnt Norton,* glances at the concept of time in which past and future meet in the present and create the vicious circle of sin and its repetition:

If all time is eternally present
All time is unredeemable.

This leads to the idea of time in individual life where the beginning is the happy garden of childhood, 'moving without pressure, over the dead leaves'. The second movement states the concept of the reconciliation of the opposites, the rhythm of tension in the external world as propounded by Heraclitus:

Garlic and saphires in the mud
Clot the bedded axle-tree.
The trilling wire in the blood
Sings below inveterate scars
Appeasing long-forgotten wars.
....
We move above the moving tree
In light upon the figured leaf
And hear upon the sodden floor
Below, the boarhound and the boar
  Pursue their pattern as before
But reconciled among the stars.

This naturally leads to the spiritual reconciliation in a higher philosophical state attained by man in momentary ecstasy and illumination of mind:

At the still point of the turning world.
Neither flesh nor fleshless;
Neither from nor towards; at the still point, there the dance is,
But neither arrest nor movement. And do not call it fixity,
Where past and future are gathered......
Except for the point, the still point,
There would be no dance, and there is only the dance.

This is the state known as *'dvandvātīta'*, transcendence of opposites in Indian *Vedānta:*

The release from action and suffering, release from the inner
And the outer compulsion, yet surrounded
By a grace of sense, a white light still and moving
Erhebung without motion, concentration
Without elimination, both a new world
And the old made explicit, understood.

This is a state above the 'twittering world', the 'way up of St. John of the Cross. But there is an opposite way also, the way of renunciation, depletion of sensuous love and desires, a withdrawal into the solitude of one's own soul:

Descend lower, descend only
Into the world of perpetual solitude,
World, not world, but that which is not world.
Internal darkness, deprivation
And destitution of all property,
Desiccation of the world of sense,
Evacuation of the world of fancy
Inoperancy of the world of spirit.

This in the state attained only momentarily in contemplation and artistically in composition where the flux of words is arrested in a permanent harmony:

Only by the form, the pattern,
Can words or music reach
The stillness, as a Chinese jar still
Moves perpetually in stillness.

From words we come to *Word*, the Logos, Christ in wilderness, assailed by temptations which ultimately melt into the thin air:

The Word in the desert
Is most attacked by voices of temptation,
The crying shadow of the funeral dance,
The loud lament of the disconsolate chimera.

In *East Coker* the starting point is the union of opposites, life and death forming the rhythm of nature and of human existence. The harmony between man and woman in dance, a homely symbol of 'Dung and death'—'In my beginning is my end'. Then comes the contrast between the wisdom provided by secular history and the wisdom of the devout:

Do not let me hear
Of the wisdom of old men, but rather of their folly,
Their fear of fear and frenzy, their fear of possession
Of belonging to another, or to others, or to God.
The only wisdom we hope to acquire
Is the wisdom of humility: humility is endless.

The third section opens with 'O dark dark dark'—darkness of blind Samson, which melts into the darkness of London underground and on the surface of society and in the mind of man and ends with an implication of the blind Milton's resignation to God whieh is the way, open to all, for emergence into light:

I said to my soul, be still, and let the dark come upon you
Which shall be the darkness of God.
Wait without thought, for you are not ready for thought:
So the darkness shall be the light, and the stillness the dancing.

This naturally leads to the idea of suffering as the legacy of Christ, "The Wounded Surgeon', who probes poignantly into the diseased soul for its own health:

The dripping blood our only drink,
The bloody flesh our only food:
In spite of which we like to think
That we are sound, substantial blood.

The is the wisdom which the old men must learn:

We must be still and still moving
Into another intensity
For a further union and deeper communion
Through the dark cold and the empty desolation.

The Dry Salvages introduces the theme of time and eternity, history, personal and of the race, symbolized as river and sea, flux and permanence, chaos and the order to which it may be reduced:

It seems as one becomes older
That the past has another pattern, and ceases to be a mere sequence.

This pattern is glimpsed in a moment of 'sudden illumination' 'which is not the experience of one life only but of many generations:

We appreciate this better in the agony of others
Involving ourselves than in our own.

Thus, 'time the destroyer is time the preserver', because 'People change, and smile, but agony abides'. Man, the voyager, should reach 'a still point' and 'consider the future and the past with equal mind'. This is detached action or inaction preached by Krishna to Arjuna:

Not fare well,
But fare forward, voyager.

To explore the meaning of history is the job of curious men and women of the world, but to apprehend

The point of intersection of timeless
With time, is the occupation for the saint.

This is the point of the impossible union: Here the past and future

Are conquered and reconciled.

This union is most dramatically symbolized by the concept of Incarnation, Word becoming flesh and linking heaven with earth, God with man. This is a good warrant for even the mortal of no saintly disposition for a life-long devotion and discipline, to be able to attain to an intuition, however momentary, of the order underlying the apparent chaos of life:

For most of us, there is only the unattended
Moment, the moment in and out of time
The distraction fit, lost in a shaft of sunlight
......or music heard so deeply
That it is not heard at all, but you are the music
While the music lasts.

The fourth poem, *Little Gidding,* shows the way of resolution and transmutation of suffering through-prayer and religious discipline in terms of Christian religion and mysticism. The starting point is the remark of Lord Krishṇa that 'what a person desires at the time of his death' goes a long way in shaping his next life, which is alluded to in the closing section of the preceding poem. It means that the past can play a crucial part in determining the present and the past may become 'eternal present' if we have the right way of looking at history. There are, in the life-cycles of the race many 'timeless moments', that is, moments of which the significance is eternal, which, like Wordsworthian 'spots of time', have the power to feed and nourish the famished spirit of the race. One such incident in English history is the visit of King Charles I to the small Church at Little Gidding at a time of great crisis and suffering. The incident is at once temporal and timeless, and the poet is anxious to underline this point:

> Here, the intersection of the timeless moment
> Is England and no where. Never and always.

The dead past is the most potent teacher of the so-called living present:

> The communication
> Of the dead is tongued with fire, beyond the language of the living.

The 'tongue of fire' introduces us to 'the dark dove with a flickering tongue' and the scene changes to London during the second world war under the rain of fire from German planes. The agonized poet is trying to find out a meaning in this meaningless brutality of human mind gone mad. He naturally summons the 'compound ghost' of the past, a representative of the European culture apparently dead to us, for this purpose. He also was eoncerned with speech, and speech 'impelled us to purify the dialect of the tribe and urge the mind to after sight and hind sight'.

The speaker proceeds to 'disclose the gifts reserved for the age, as body and soul begin to fall asunder', and the soul is conditioned for the deeper insight:

> From wrong to wrong the exasperated spirit
> Proceeds, unless restored by that refining fire
> Where you must move in measure, like a dancer`.

The 'blitz' must be accepted as 'a fire of purgatory to redeem its meaning in the life of suffering humanity'. If you use history this way to resolve the problems of to-day, history may be a source of liberation:

> To become renewed, transfigured, in another pattern.

So the fire-breathing dove becomes the Holy Ghost, with its clarion-call to tormented humanity;

> The one discharge from sin and error,
> The only hope, or else despair
> Lies in the choice of pyre or pyre...........
> To be redeemed from fire by fire.

Turn the flame of hate and lust into the fire of purgatory, replace the languid ecstasy of flesh by self-imposed denial and mortification, for a true devotee suffering is the rough and bruising embrace of God's love which tortures the soul into divine perfection:

> Love is the unfamiliar Name
> Behind the hands that wove
> The intolerable shirt of flame
> Which human power cannot remove.

The resolution,, however, is a determined effort to regain the state of mind and soul which charcterized us at the beginning of our career—childhood in the case of the individual and the happy garden state for our common Adam:

> We shall not cease from exploration
> And the end of our exploring
> Will be to arrive where we started
> And know the place for the first time.

The *Four Quartets* mark the highest point of fusion between meditative profundity and lyrical beauty and intensity in the maturest poetry of Eliot. Their movement is an upward thrust from the earth in the first poem to fire in the last and the problems of redemption of time and meaning of history posed in *Burnt Norton* are happily resolved in *Little Gidding*.

CHANGING PATTERN OF STYLE AND IMAGERY

We may now briefly summarize the basic difference in style and diction between the early and the late poems of Eliot. In the interest of brevity I prefer to quote the words of critics more competent than myself in this respect:

"The early poems show us 'the immense panorama of futility and anarchy which is contemporary history'......the moods of ironic and cynical repulsion, of unromantic disillusionment and of nervous intensity......There is the impact on the senses of all the ugliness and squalor of the common urban scene; the sights of the broken blinds and Chimney pots, of vacant lots with their grimy scraps of newspapers etc. Above all there are the smells, of steak in passage-ways, of stale beer, of cocktails and cigarettes, of dusty paper-flowers, of female in shuttered rooms" (Elizabeth Drew,)

"In his later poetry instead of looking out upon the world and seeing sharply defined and various manifestations of the same desolation and emptiness, the poet turns away from the outer world of men to ponder over certain intimate personal experiences. His verse moves into another intensity. The new imagery lacks the sharp precision as well as realism of the earlier. The images are mostly beautiful and poetically suggestive in themselves. They are often drawn from nature......Many of the images are traditional, common symbols which have an age-old meaning—the rose, the garden, the fountain, the desert, the Yew......the poet mingles this imagery with images of natural beauty and with more esoteric images: the white leopards, the jewelled unicorns, the aged eagle......and the fluteplayer in blue and green." To this may be added the religious and mystic symbols more or less conventional yet charged with new life and intensity in the *Four Quartets*—the turning wheel and the still-point, the stairs of ascent, dance, dark night of the soul etc.

"Eliot's most striking quality of poetry that culminates in *The Waste Land* was an extreme power of condensation. Whether in the free rhymed verse, or in quatrains, or in the blank verse of

Gerontion, his poetry had a peculiar force of expression; it was economical of words, omitting the merely connecting phrase, elliptical and in the best sense rhetorical."

(Helen Gardner).

"The later poetry sheds off all the surface incrustations and becomes luminously transparent without losing the density of texture. It is relaxed, supple, incantatory and repetitious, and poignantly lyrical. The liberation is not only outer but also inner, a sense of release from the prison-house, a vigour of emotional energy bursting the covering of reticence and coldness of heart, under the pressure of deeply-felt sentiments.

"Instead of dramatic clashes and startling associations and references which require constant elucidation from outside the poems, the language itself penetrates more and more deeply into the structure, word becomes more and more loaded with meaning. It is squeezed and squeezed of every drop of its juice. It is ex-pression at its fullest."

E. Drew.

Eliot thus started, perhaps under the influence of his friend and mentor, Ezra Pound, combined with his own early revulsion against the diffuseness and verbal debauch of the decadent Romantic style, with a poetry of studied difficulty and self-conscious isolation from the circle of common readers, which justified the criticism of Prof. Laski. But his conviction about the social aim of poetry in subsequent years induced him to simplify his manner in order to share his valuable feelings and experiences with as wide an audience as possible, The point is emphasized by him in one of his representative critical passages where he discusses the necessity, the nature and utility of the dramatic communication:

> "The most useful poetry, socially, would be one which could cut across all the present stratifications of public taste—stratifications which are perhaps a sign of social disintegration. The ideal medium for poetry, to my mind, and the most direct means of social 'usefulness' for poetry is the theatre".

Yet the complaint has been voiced and regret expressed in certain quarters that, in his later poetry, the poet occupied himself solely with religious themes and motives and thereby narrowed the range of his poetic appeal. I, for one, find little justification for the attitude of those people who shut their ears as soon as a poet begins to talk of God, Incarnation, Sin, Repentance and Salvation, foregtting the most essential fact that these words are only symbols of some of the deepest and most intimate needs and experiences of humanity and, as such, are ever old but always young. If the 'dirty' years of our industrial age are deaf to them, the blame does not lie with the poet, who, quite properly, resolved to purge the heart of his people by means of what he felt to be the sacred wisdom of the ages.

Yet religious poetry imposes certain limitations which Eliot himself has described perceptively:

"The religious poet is not a poet who is treating the whole subject matter of poetry in a religious spirit, but a poet who is dealing with a confined part of this subject matter: who is leaving out what men consider their major passions and thereby confessing his ignorance of them." (Selected Essays: p. 390).

Such a poet is more inclined to perceive the boredom and horror of the ordinary life rather than its beauty and glory and for him the world will not be a place of exhilarating struggles and noble achievements, but a large hospital where the sick souls may find the sole hope of their healing in the acceptance of suffering. Eliot is emphatic on this point in his essay on Dante 'that poetry not only must be found through suffering but can find its material only in suffering". This severe discipline bred in him a detachment which Coleridge has aptly described in relation to Wordsworth :

"His proper title is spectator *ab extra*. Although he is capable of the most profound sympathy 'with man as man', his is the sympathy of a contemplator rather than a fellow-sufferer". None, therefore, was better fitted to prick the bubbles of our progress-intoxicated age than the author of *Gerontion* and *The Waste Land*:

The endless cycle of idea and action,
Endless invention, endless experiment
Brings knowledge of motion, but not of stillness
Knowledge of speech, but not of silence;
Knowledge of words, and ignorance of the Word.
The cycles of Heaven in twenty centuries
Bring us farther from God and nearer to the Dust.

SECTION II

THE WASTE LAND

THE WASTE LAND

(I)

The year 1922 may, in a special sense, be regarded as a land-mark in the history of the 20th-century English literature, as it witnessed, among other things, the publication of two masterpieces, James Joyce's *Ulysses* and Eliot's *The Waste Land*, which emphatically proclaimed the birth of the modernist 'Minerva in full panoply', the maturing of a literature permeated with the complexity and self-consciousness of the contemporary thought and sensibility. Critics have dwelt upon the striking similarities between the two and have pointed out obvious echoes of Joyce in Eliot, and the latter himself has left us in little doubt about the keenness of his own interest in the venture of the fellow historian of modern consciousness and pitiless dissector of the spiritual degration and moral chaos which characterized the European society, surviving the shattering effect of the World War I, only by the skin of its teeth. The condition of this society has been put, in a nut-shell, by D. H. Lawrence, another prophet of the age, in his *Kangaroo*: "It was in 1915 that the old world ended. In the winter of 1915-16 the spirit of the old London collapsed; the city in some way perished, perished from being the heart of the world, and became a vortex of broken passions, lusts, hopes and fears and horrors."

Joyce, however, adopted the technique of expansion and elaboration, multiplying the events of a single day in the life of his protagonist to produce a novel of epic magnitude, while Eliot followed the opposite method of compression and telescoping, so that the human predicament in the contemporary history gets linked with that in other ages of human civilization and the malaise under observation is turned into the eternal problem of man; the past and the present merge together and antiquity is brought into the embrace of contemporaneity, and all this in a poem of 434 lines. In a well-known article in the *Dial,* Eliot had the perspicacity to single out one aspect of Joyce's technique for special commendation as a step fraught with fruitful possibilities for contemporary practitioners of the literary craft:

> "In using the myth, in manipulating a continuous parallel between contemporaneity and antiquity, Mr. Joyce is pursuing a method which others must pursue after him...It is simply a way of controlling, of ordering, of giving a shape and a significance to the immense panorama of futility and anarchy which is contemporary history".

This 'mythical method' is the key to the understanding of the apparently 'formless' form of *The Waste Land,* where a myth is used as a norm of order and harmony in the human life in antiquity, to measure the extent of moral confusion and spiritual chaos in the post-war European society on which attention is focussed. The method thus underlines not only 'the pastness of the past but also its presence'; it views the contemporary human problem as a repetition and continuation of a permanent problem of humanity, while emphasizing everywhere the wide gulf which separates the godless humanity of to-day from the early human society when moral and spiritual values were intact to guide the human destiny and redeem man from the career of sin and crime.

Eliot was in full agreement with the current discoveries of the Anthropologists and the Psychologists that the old myths were the repository of human wisdom and human crises and represented the first successful attempt of primitive humanity to bring its life into a fruitful relationship with the external forces, natural as well as supernatural, and in the 'notes' added to the poems, he frankly acknowledges his indebtedness to Frazer's *The Golden Bough* and Miss Weston's *From Ritual to Romance*, both of which have emphasized a common pattern recurrent in the series of old myths and subsequently adopted in the mystery-cults and by Christianity itself. This pattern may be described as the theme of death and re-birth, of the loss of life followed by its renewal. In the old nature-myths the pattern centres round winter, as the death of the year, followed by spring, the season when the current of life courses again through the frozen anatomy of Nature. The same pattern runs through the fertility myths which celebrated the loss of the land's fertility in the season of drought, betokening death, and its return with rains, the harbinger of the rebirth of the dead land. The process was enacted in the particular rituals connected with the burial of the vegetation god, which was quickly followed by his coming back to life again. The effigy of the god was stuck with grains all over the body and then buried in the earth. After a few days the grains sprouted and green blades broke into the light of the day. The dead god was reborn. The process was spiritualized in the mystery cults where the initiate had to undergo a terrible ordeal and to die in body so that he may have a rebirth in spirit. Finally this recurring pattern of death and rebirth was taken over by Christianity and assimilated with its central myth—the crucifixion and resurrection of Christ, the Saviour, who was sent to this earth to redeem mankind from the sin of Adam, 'which brought death into the world and all our woes.'

Apart from this central motif there is a repeated emphasis, in these myths, upon the most intimate connection between sex and religion, the sanctity of sex forming the base, as it were, of the health and vitality of spiritual life and its violation serving as a manifestation of the decay of the religious instinct. On the physical plane sex was sanctified in marriage, in the lawful and regulated union of man and woman for procreation, so necessary for the preservation and multiplication of the human race. But the sexual union had to be sublimated in the higher union between the soul of man and his Creator. It has been rightly pointed out that the Cup and the Lance in the Grail legend are sexual symbols and so are the emblems on the Tarot packs used in Egypt and other countries in the performance of the fertility rituals.

In the well-known passage in *Hamlet* criticism, Eliot has enjoined upon the poet the supreme necessity of escaping his private emotions and his own personality by getting hold of an 'Objective Correlative', that is, some event, incident or situation which may become an appropriate formula for his emotion, so that given the situation, the emotion may become articulated automatically. In *The Waste Land* the 'Objective Correlative' is formed by the mediaeval myth of the Fisher King, which is connected with the famous Grail legend. The Grail was, initially, the dish or plate used by Christ in the Last Supper, in which the blood of the saviour was held up on the eve of his Crucifixion by one of his devotees. It was not long before this holy vessel was discovered to have acquired medicinal and miraculous properties so that it became an object of devotion and worship and temples came to be built in several countries and its worship was organized. But a time came when the Grail disappeared mysteriously and many a bold Knight staked his life and lost it in the arduous task of its quest and re-discovery. It was generally believed that the lost Grail sometimes appeared in the sky as a floating saucer of great beauty and splendour, but it could be seen only by a Knight of virginal purity. Tennyson treated of this theme as the finale of his *Idylls of the King*, making Sir Galahad, the immaculate Knight of King Arthur's Round Table, as the leader destined to succeed in his holy mission. In other versions appearing subsequently in Germany and France, however, the protagonist is Sir Perceival or Parsifal. Miss Weston, in her *From Ritual to Romance,* one of the source-books for the author of *The Waste Land,* has treated the legend critically and historically and has concluded that the Grail was originally connected with the fertility myth, as is witnessed by its sexual symbols, but later it suffered a sea-change with its association with the founder of Christianity.

It is said that in the course of their hazardous quest Parsifal and his fellow adventurers happened to arrive in a country ruled over by a prince, named The Fisher King, It was one of the regions where Grail worship had been anciently in vogue and a temple, known as Chapel Perilous, still stood there, broken and dilapidated, as a mournful memorial of what once was but later had ceased to be. At that time the King himself had become a human wreck, maimed and impotent, as a result, it was whispered, of a sin committed by his soldiery in outraging the modesty of a group of nuns attached to the Grail temple. The impotency of the Fisher King was reflected sympathetically in the land of which he was the head and the ruler, which had become dry and barren, the haunt and home of want and famine. The King, however, was waiting with hope despite despair, that one day the Knight of the pure soul would visit his star-crossed kingdom, march to the Chapel Perilous, answer questions and solve riddles prior to the ritual washing of his sinful body, which would purge it and renew its health and energy, and this rebirth of the king would be a signal for the advent of the life-giving rains to the parched land and the thirsty kingdom which would once more be decked with 'soft incense' and 'lisping leaves'.

This is the legend of the Fisher King and his mythical Waste Land, a fit analogue for the modern kingdom of spiritual sterility and moral decay, where love is turned into lust and union between man and woman has become blindly instinctual like the coupling of animals. The impotent Fisher King symbolizes humanity to-day as well as in any age of history, when the spiritual current has ebbed and life is reduced to the animal plane, 'birth, copulation and death' and man has forgotten his noble ancestry, that he was made 'in the image of God' and framed above the shows of the earth and above the circle of animal existence. This is the condition of his death and his salvation lies in his success to rise above his senses, his animal instincts and desires, divesting himself of all that the world can give in order to be invested with the light and life of the spirit.

The Structure of the Poem

The structure of *The Waste Land* is not progressive but rather circular; it does not tell a story which moves through well-marked stages to a destined goal but explores the significance of certain themes presented symbolically, turning round and round them till the last drop of meaning is squeezed out of them without any the least recourse to direct statement or assertion. In musical terms its is a symphony of five inter-connected movements, where the various aspects of the theme or various symbols stand like different instruments or keys, each with its own tune, which, however, form a part of the larger harmony of the general music. That Eliot may have consciously designed the poem on the musical pattern is borne out by his own critical remarks which clearly reflect his preoccupation with this technique. We have space only for one representative quotation from his lecture on *The Music of Poetry*:

> "The use of recurrent themes is as natural to poetry as to music; there are possibilities for verse which bear some analogy to the development of a theme by different groups of instruments; there are possibilities of transition in a poem comparable to the different movements of a symphony or quartet; there are possibilities of contrapuntal arrangement of subject-matter".

We shall have occasion to illustrate these points in the course of our detailed analysis of the various sections of the poem, but such an analysis should be preceded by a brief explanation of the significance of Tiresias, the protagonist of the poem and its unifying symbol.

TIRESIAS

Tiresias, according to Eliot, is the central figure in the poem, an interested spectator of the modern wasteland, and 'what Tiresias sees is the substance of the whole poem'. The significance of Tiresias is complex and varied. Historically he is connected with the story of King Oedipus of Thebes, which is clearly and demonstrably the classical legend of wasteland, with striking resemblances to the drought-infested, sin-ridden kingdom of the Mediaeval Fisher King.

In this way the introduction of Tiresias serves, in the first place, to complicate the mythical frame of the poem, to universalize its central significance by bringing home to us the enormity of sin involved in the violation of the sanctity of sex and the necessity of purifying the sinner's soul through suffering as the sole way to salvation. Oedipus unwittingly kills his father and marries his own mother and thus calls down upon his supposedly innocent head the curse of the gods in the form of a virulent plague, epidemic and destructive, which neither King nor commoner fails to regard as a nemesis for some dark and hidden crime. Tiresias, the blind prophet, is summoned and compelled by the King's obdurate pride to tell the shocking truth that he himself is the plague-spot. Such is the conspiracy of circumstances that the King is slowly but irresistibly driven to the realization of this horrible truth. Nothing remains for the king but the duty of expiation, self-mutilation, self-exile, self-abasement and a prolonged penance and self-immolation which eventually generate spiritual calm and inner illumination. But the symbolic significance of Tiresias is much more important in this poem. He is bi-sexual with a fuller experience of life than any normal man or woman and his physical blindness is more than compensated by his prophetic vision. He is the fittest symbol of human consciousness itself, the accumulated experience and knowledge of the race acquired during its long and devious passage through the immense stretch of time. He is the enlightened ghost of the race watching the depressing spectacle of modern humanity which has fallen from the ancient heights and forgotten the old values and sanctities. But he is at once a relic of the past and a scion of the present, at once a prophet and detached spectator of the agonizing drama in contemporary history and a participator and fellow-sufferer, with a superior insight into the meaning of the ghostly masquerade, miscalled 'human life'. Psychologically speaking he is the conscience of humanity, banished and disowned by thoughtless men and women but still strong enough to prick the bubbles of their illusions, joys, hopes and fears. His is the voice of sensitive humanity deploring the depletion of spirituality in the modern world and probing into the strange disease which it has, with criminal complacency, mistaken for its health. His lynx-eyed vision pierces through this thin veneer of complacency and lays bare the sordid cares and languid pursuits, the boredom and sheer vacuity to which humanity in the modern wasteland has fallen a prey. Tiresias, thus, is a complex and protean persona or symbol and supplies whatever unity the poem may be discovered to have. But for his presence throughout the poem it would have become a phantasmagoria, a nightmare, a medley of scenes and meaningless snatches of talk almost overwhelming in its confused impression. Eliot himself has explicitly, though succinctly, stated the vital significance of Tiresias' role in the poem:

> "Tiresias although a mere spectator and not indeed a character, is yet the most important personage in the poem, uniting all the rest. Just as the one-eyed merchant, seller of currants, melts into the Phoenician Sailor, and the latter is not wholly distinct from Ferdinand, Prince of Naples, so all the women are one woman, and the two sexes meet in Tiresias".

As a symbol of the past still surviving in the present, the old man with 'wrinkled female breast' Tiresias 'has foresuffered all 'that is being enacted on the ugly stage of the contemporary world and is, therefore, competent enough to effect the merger of the past and the present and underline, at the same time, the moral gulf that yawns between them.

The poem may best be regarded as a long and complex cinema film, transcending the barrier of time and place with swift flashes coming in succession but illuminating now a scene in the present and then an incident in the past, so that mentally we are to interweave the 'now' of history with any moment, anywhere and in any period; and a scene in London with that in any modern European capital or with other places of history, near or remote. In this way a cunning fabric is contrived on the loom of art in which Time is conquered and a contemporary problem is given a universal and permanent significance. The voice of Tiresias, who easily assumes many masks, alternates with the voices in the modern wasteland and at times with the ghostly voices of the past. If Spenser creates a dream world in his *Faerie Queene,* Eliot contrives to conjure up a nightmare in *The Waste Land.* But the nightmare, like its fairy counterpart, has a hard core of meaning which we are now in a position to explore and elucidate.

(II)

Before we enter upon this intellectual exploration we must briefly pause at the epigraph on the title page which is obviously drawn from the *Satyricon* of Petronius and refers to a significant colloquy between a drunken scoffer and the most celebrated prophetess of antiquity, the Sybil of Cumae, who was granted by Apollo the boon of an immensely long life without the permanence of youth and naturally shrank up into a thin spectre in course of time. The drunken scoffer finds this Sibyl of Cumae hanging in a cage and breathing from time to time the secret longing of her heart in the cryptic but pregnant remark, wish to die'. This motto of the poem contains the sum and essence of its primary theme, because it reflects, on the surface, the death-wish of modern humanity, its willingness to exist merely on the animal plane in total disregard for the spiritual life, but it also points ambivalently to the duty of man to die physically in order to be able to live spiritually, to deprive himself gradually of all worldliness so that he may in time advance from the realm of death to the luminous life of the soul. 'Lead me from death unto immortality' is the well-known Indian prayer which illustrates our point.

It is, thus, clear that the poem moves between the physical life, which is the death of the spirit, and physical death (the negation of the senses) which is a necessary stage in the re-birth of the soul, the spiritual regeneration of man when he gets above the torture of the desire unfulfilled and the greater torment of the desire fulfilled, 'the sad satiety' of love.

The Burial of the Dead

The opening section or the first movement of the poeem is entitled 'The Burial of the Dead', which refers to the burial of the dead fertility gods described by Frazer and others and the burial service for the dead performed in the Christian Church. In both the cases death is believed to be followed by re-birth or resurrection, This process is contrasted with conditions in the modern waste-land where the possibility of re-birth has become problematical and humanity has surrendered itself to a way of life which is acually a living-death. Thus, the first section places before us the pivotal points—death, life-in-death and re-birth of the soul round which the whole poem revolves.

The opening lines, 'April is the cruellest month' etc. represent the meditation of Tiresias, the Protagonist, who is reflecting upon the life in the modern wasteland, like some Biblical prophet contemplating a sinful scene. Yet he speaks like a representative of this humanity, gifted only with a superior acumen to attempt a frank appraisal of its peculiar psychology. It is the month of April, the life-giving showers have fertilized the dead womb of the earth and stirred the inert roots into activity, so that nature has resumed the lapsed process of birth and growth, and the beautiful lilac flowers have begun to appear on the surface, piercing through the grave-like darkness in the barren bowels of the earth. This is the return of life, the mixing of memory and desire, connecting the past with the present and thus restoring the rhythm of life in nature which was broken by dead winter. Yet this process of re-birth out of death is extremely painful and beyond the endurance of the timid and light-hearted denizens of the wasteland, who are content to cling to winter and find warmth there even though it means life at the lowest ebb, a mere breathnig, not real living. The pain of re-birth in spring is described by Eliot elsewhere also:

> The ache in the moving root
> The agony in the dark
> The slow flow throbbing in the trunk
> The pain of the breaking bud
> The wail of the new full tide
> Returning the ghosts of the dead
> Those whom the winter drowned.
>
> (*Family Reunion*)

In the life of man also re-birth is as painful as death isself. The speaker in Eliot's '*Journey of the Magi*' testifies to this fact: 'This birth was a hard and bitter agony for us, like death, our death, we wish to die'. This remark reminds us of an illuminating observation of Jung in *Psychological Types* (p. 328): 'The birth of a deliverer is equivalent to a great catastrophe since a new and powerful life issues forth just when no life or force or new development was anticipated. This reversal of values is tantamount to a destruction of previously accepted values: hence it resembles a devastation', The implication of the remark is applicable to all new births out of death.

Behind this 'cruellest April' of Eliot there lurks the spring with the 'shoures swete' in the opening of Chaucer's *Prologue* to the *Canterbury Tales*. The contrast is obvious and deliberate and quite crucial at this juncture. The sweetness of Chaucer's spring lies in the fact that it brought about a double birth, the flood-tide of life in nature and an acute stirring of faith in the heart of man. Amid bursting boughs and tuneful warblings men started on their pilgrimage, talking and singing and telling entertaining tales—'Go' 'Go' sang the bird among the branches and 'Come' 'Come' whispered the saint from his shrine, the wave of life in nature and the tide of faith in man met in a happy confluence and made the spring a really sweet season. But in the modern wasteland 'April is the cruellest month' because the renewal of life in the universe of nature appears a cruel mockery of the deadness of humanity lying contentedly in the sleep inducing lap of the winter. This Winter is the symbol of spiritual death, a living on the surface of existence —eating, sleeping, breeding and clutching at the momentary pleasures within reach—without regret for the past and fear or desire for the future—'take the cash in hand and waive the rest—the infirm glory of a positive hour'. This winter contrasts with 'April', symbol of spiritual rebirth, which mixes 'memory and desire' the past and the future with the present of man, thus making him quite worthy of himself, a creature, in the words of Hamlet, 'of large discourse, looking before and after'. For a spiritually sound man, however, memory and desire are something more than mere mundane concern. His memory may go back to Eden, the Garden of Paradise, where man once lived and which he lost through his sin of disobedience, while his 'desire' may be fixed on the ultimate goal of man, which is to 'regain the blissful seat.' The spiritual pilgrimage of man is actually a retreat, the way forward is the movement backward, the final aim being only to reach the point from which the parents of mankind, Adam and Eve, started, 'hand in hand' but weeping, into the space, dark and wide, which opened before their confused vision.

These meditative lines are followed by a light-hearted chat between two creatures of the waste-land for whom summer and winter are mere seasons and life is a movement from cold north to warm south in search of recreation and physical comfort, romance and new sensations. The speaker is a German princess, (I am no Russian; I come from Lithuania, a true German who can speak German and English fluently but is a rolling stone, a globe-trotter, with no permanent habitation. She is a fit symbol of rootless internationalism, the worst enemy of sound culture and morality. Eliot has reminded us, again and again, that the real life, spiritual and moral, can be developed only in a well-organized community, with its roots deep into the soil:

> There is no life that is not in community
> And no community not lived in praise of God.

The German princess has no communal and religious ties and naturally for her summer showers and sunshines are only literal things regarded good or bad in terms solely of her physical comfort and discomfort. She is surprised by summer with a sudden shower of rain and takes shelter to avoid drenching. She has no sense of the spiritual significance of rain and water—the fertilizing, purifying and transforming property of water as reflected in ritual immersion, baptism and drowning etc. Her memory and desires also are physical and mundane—the memory of her childhood with her cousin, the Archduke, who sustained her failing courage while riding a sledge and the desire to go to the South, the warmer climate, where one feels more free, not certainly for spiritual adventure and exaltation but for amorous sports and surrender to romance.

After this talk of spring and summer we move on to the picture of spiritual winter in the waste-land. Like some prophet of the Old Testament the Protagonist surveys the wide panorama of spiritual chaos, futility and fragmentation and asks in a tone of bewilderment if it is possible for anything to take root and grow (spiritually, of course) in a soil which has become so inhospitable to any thought of spirituality. It is 'stony rubbish', a society not only spiritually barren, but utterly disorganized, uprooted and littered with the wrecks of the old ideals and values. The puzzled prophet, 'son of man' (as the biblical prophet was designated by the angel of God in *Ezekiel*, for example), gets the answer from a superior voice to the effect that so far as spiritual re-birth and growth in this decaying society is concerned it is difficult even to make any hopeful guess. One can be certain only of its increasing barrenness, degeneration and utter spiritual destitution. In these lines, it is not difficult to see that the physical landscape, with stony rocks breaking under the scorching sun, the dead tree denuded of its shady foliage and stony soil in the deadening grip of drought, without even the sound of water, is the symbol of the stark spiritual barrenness without the least trace of the quickening of the soul. The 'heap of broken images' lying around are the debris of shattered values, creeds and conventions which once served as the guiding principles of human life and accounted for the integrity of the individual and the solidarity of the community of which he was a living part, 'a shady tree' fruitful in himself and beneficial to others ! We may refer to Isaiah's prophecy, 'a man shall be as rivers of water in a dry place, as the shadow of a great rock in a weary land'. The passage is charged with biblical phraseology and oblique allusions and echoes which enrich the meaning and the associational implications of the lines. Here is a biblical passage from *Ecclesiastes,* with the same haunting rhythm: 'When they shall be afraid of that which is high, and fear shall be in the way, and the almond tree shall flourish, and the grasshopper shall be a burden, and desire shall fail, because man goeth to his long home and the mourners go about the streets'. The keyword in the passage is 'fear' which throws an interesting light on the passage following, where the prophet is invited to come under the shadow of the 'red-rock' where he will be shown 'fear in a handful of dust', that is, in the soulless humanity which has denied its God. The 'red-rock' has been described by many commentators as an obscure phrase quite intriguing in the context, though pregnant with the implications of terror. The word 'red' has the soul of terror, which is intensified by the other contexts in the poem where it occurs. In the fifth movement, for example, we have 'Torch-light *red* on sweaty faces', and the '*red* sullen faces that sneer and snarl'. The suggestion of anger and terror is quite apparent here. Then the word 'red' recalls the idea of curse as a punishment for sin in Coleridge's *Ancient Mariner:*

> But where the ship's dark shadow lay
> The charmed water burnt alway
> A still and awful *red.*

So 'red' combined with 'rock', which is a conventional symbol for God, envisions the image of the angry God sitting in judgement, as it were, over the sinful humanity in our wasteland. The descriptions of the scene of God's judgement all point to the condition of panic and fear in the human multitude, when men will seek the coverings of the mountains to escape the wrath of the Divine Judge. We recall the biblical warning: 'Enter into the rock, and hide in the dust, for fear of the Lord, and for the glory of his majesty'. The godless humanity of to-day, however, is absolutely unaware of God, sin and divine punishment, still the effect of sin lies heavy on it, as it is haunted by fear. The shadow under the 'red-rock' is timeless and is clearly contrasted with the shadow which strides behind man in the morning and advances to meet him in the evening. This shadow is the symbol of man's mortality which accompanies him throughout his life, with the only difference that in youth (morning) it lies behind, while life opens out in front of him, while in old age (evening) the shadow of death comes before and advances menacingly to arrest his movement. But the 'fear in a handful of dust' to be shown to the protagonist is something different from this common doom of the mortal creation. It is the fear which haunts man between his 'morning' and his 'evening', as Davies, the Georgian poet, has happily put it—From his cradle to his grave the poor devil, man, is haunted with fear. This fear arises alike out of our joys and our sorrows, our hopes and our disappointments.

The idea, therefore, sheds light upon the two scenes of love, one taken from a modern German opera and the other referring to a momentary ecstasy in the 'Hyacinth garden'. The German extract is cited from Wagner's musical play *Tristan and Isolde*, the famous mediaeval story of guilty love, which has inspired a good many poems and prose-works in Europe. The song has been rendered in English as 'fresh blows the wind from homeland, my Irish child, where are you tarrying ?' This is the beginning of the guilty love between Tristan and Isolde, with all the ecstasy and torture of the forbidden fruit, which ended, however, in unspeakable agony with Tristan, the broken lover, waiting for his beloved's arrival on the sea-shore, but 'empty and blank the sea', no trace of the eagerly waited-for ship with its precious freight. It is remarkable that the last line of the German fragment—'empty and blank the sea'—is given at the end of the second episode, the confession of the lover of the Hyacinth girl, which means that the two contrasted episodes of ecstatic love have the same effect—a momentary joy followed by regret, pain and fear. The second is a beautiful episode with the picture of the young girl, with an armful of Hyacinths, cooled and refreshed by the dew drops. It is the picture of youthful love (symbolised by the Hyacinth) with an obvious reference to the fertility festival. The girl standing, as Miss Elizabeth Drew has pointed out, for 'spring and abundance and an exquisite promise'. What the lover is describing is a momentary ecstasy, when a person is 'neither flesh nor fleshless', when the senses fail and stop functioning and the spirit soars up to heavenly bliss. 'Silence in the heart of light', the image from Dante's *Paradiso*—'from the heart of one of the new lights'—supplies the most telling epitome of this state. The garden image of ecstatic early love is so recurrent in Eliot that some critics have been led to believe that the poet was drawing upon a personal memory of happy but frustrated love, like that between Arnold and Marguerite, but who the Marguerite of Eliot was is difficult to decide. But I personally have a strong suspicion that in this description also there is an undercurrent of the sense of guilt and the man's momentary blindness recalls to our mind the well-known fact that men of impure heart were struck blind by the vision of the Grail and could not see it. The episode is reminiscent of the innocent and ecstatic love between Ferdinand and Miranda in *The Tempest,* where Prospero, with his magic, is able to overpower the prince and render him quite immobile when he offers to resist him. But there also the young lovers have to be reminded again and again that the consummation of love before their lawful union in marriage will be a sin and must be avoided. If this reading of the two episodes is correct, then one cannot help recalling Eliot's comment on Baudelaire's distinction between the sexual relation between man and woman, which is based upon the moral sense of good and evil and the mere coupling of beasts which is prompted by natural instinct alone without any moral implication. So these love-episodes glance ironically on all sexual unions in the wasteland, which is merely biological, a gratification of the animal urge, a sensual recreation rather than a sacramental union or even a passionate clutching at the fleshly transport.

We now move into the heart of the 'unreal city' (London here) to Madam Sosostris, the famous clairvoyante (the fortune-teller) with her 'wicked cards' known as the Tarot pack. Miss Drew has drawn our attention to this woman of dubious gift, with 'her name suggesting a Greek-Egyptian origin, who is a modern vulgarized version of the Egyptian diviners and practisers of magic, who professed to control fertility, and to forecast the rising and falling of the waters of the Nile through the Tarot cards......But what originated in a technique of mastery has become a masquerade. Her reality is dead and she practises her shady fortune-telling in an atmosphere of the fear of the police: 'one must be so careful these days', as one of her admirers puts to her companion. Her degradation is underlined in the remark that she has a bad cold and her voice is not clear.

In the 'notes' the poet has informed us that he has used the Tarot pack rather arbitrarily to suit his purpose. The purpose is demonstrably to introduce the important figures through the pictures on the cards in the hand of the Madame who is shown in the process of fortune-telling. The card known as 'the drowned Phoenician sailor' refers to the fourth 'movement' of the poem, 'Death by Water'. 'Fear death by water' and the fragmentary 'those are pearls that were his eyes' from the *Tempest*, refer to the contrasted meanings of drowning in water, one implying the purely physical plane where water is destructive of life, and the other denoting the spiritual significance of water as an element of life, purification, transformation and rebirth. Belladonna, the Lady of the Rocks, is a type of all womanhood in the wasteland, modern or ancient. She is the symbol of sexual sterility and opportunism, a lady of 'situations', of chance sexual encounters rather than of fruitful unions. Her name offers a elear contrast to that of the mother of Christ, Mary, Madonna of the Rocks, of Leonardo's painting, the lady of consolation and redemption of the sinners. The Lady of the Rocks is introduced in the Second section, *A Game of Chess*. The 'man with three staves' stands for the Fisher King himself, symbol of fallen humanity requiring for its salvation the threefold remedy stated in the last section, to give, to sympathise, to control. The 'wheel' is a complex symbol, standing at once for the Buddhistic 'Wheel of Righteousness' and the 'wheel' of the ship in the fourth section and also the 'whirl pool', the flux of life and the cycle of seasons. The Merchant is the one-eyed merchant of Smyrna in the third section, deprived of the other eye, the eye of religion and what he carries on his back was once the fertility cult which came to Europe through the agency of the Syrian traders, but now his cargo is mere merchandise, which includes 'homosexuality'. The 'Hanged man'is at once the sacrificial fertility god of Frazer and Christ Crucified, who is not to be found in the sordidly secular world of Madame Sosostris. The 'crowds of people, walking round in a ring' stand for the London crowd in the first part of the poem, dealers in files and ledgers and votaries of the desk, who are tied to the monotonous round of a negative existence. Then we have the 'hooded hordes' in the final section, multitude of war-torn humanity, wandering from pillar to post, 'ringed by flat horizon only'.

The following passage takes up the theme of the 'unreal city' and its flowing crowd and identifies the modern wasteland with 'Dante's *Inferno*. 'Unreal city' is Baudelaire's description of 'Paris', so London may be any capital in Europe. The city is 'unreal' because there is no civic life, life in community, with natural and spiritual vitality. It is 'unreal' also because it is not inhabited by living men and women, but by moving human ghosts who have nothing positive in their lives. The mantle of 'Brown Fog' deepens its unreality and produces an atmosphere, dim and hazy, like that in Dante's Limbo. Eliot here agrees with Shelley's verdict that hell is a city much like London. In this 'unreal city' a slow-moving crowd is seen passing like a flood over the London Bridge. It is the crowd of clerks and business functionaries who are the slaves of routine and time-table and keep themselves confined to the narrow circle of their business-life. They take no risks, make no moral and intellectual excursions, follow straight in the line of their nose and are law-abiding and even good by 'saving and hoarding themselves'. They are men of an over-prudent, negative way of life or, more precisely, death-in-life, and are rightly comparable to the multitude of doomed souls in Hell and Limbo, who made Dante exclaim, 'I had not thought death had undone so many'. These wretched creatures who are abashed and downcast and are repenting their sin in short, swift sighs are those 'who were never baptized' and those who were never alive; 'who lived without praise or blame and are wanted neither by Hell nor by Heaven'. The London crowd is the modern version of these souls, still encased in flesh and blood, but without the least trace of the living man in them. They are miscalled men 'as though to breathe were life'. Their business hour begins at nine, but the hand of the Church-clock always pointing to the ninth hour reminds us that the hour was the time of Christ's Passion or agony, or when he made his frantic prayer: 'O God, my God, why hast thou forsaken me' ? The implication, therefore, is two-fold, firstly, that the crowd has forgotten the Saviour and his sacrifice, and secondly, that the hour of business is also the hour of the Saviour's agony and death. In the modern world commerce which is the worship of Mammon and business which is the worship of dead routine amount ultimately to the denial of God.

Now the protagonist stops a Person in the crowd for conversation and inquiry as is done by Dante in the crowded Inferno. The person so selected is a figure of complex significance. In the first place, he is the counterpart of the person in Dante who 'through cowardice, made the great refusal'...... which means that he is a low creature of calculating prudence and sordid aim who is averse to high, noble thoughts and actions. Secondly, he has witnessed the war of 1914-18 and has also been with the protagonist at Mylae, the scene of the first

Punic War between Rome and Carthage which, like the modern world war, was a commercial war. So he is a type of humanity in ages past and in the present which is stimulated to fight and make sacrifices by material greed and cupidity. As the last line of the passage, a French quotation from Baudelaire's poem......(You know him, reader, this dainty monster, Hypocrite reader, my double, my brother) reminds us, Stetson stands for all humanity in the wasteland, where spiritual values have been sent out of courts by the aggressive spirit of business enterprise.

The conversation about the planting of the corpse and the fear of the Dog is one of the most characteristic passages in the poem from the view-point of meaning as well as of poetic technique. It is an emphatic illustration of the way in which Eliot adapts a quotation to his own context and completely transforms it while managing to keep the original meaning reverberating, however faintly, behind the new implication extracted out of it. Thus, the original line of the song in Webster's *White Devil* reads as, 'keep the wolf far thence that is foe to man'. Eliot has changed the inimical wolf into the friendly dog, with capital 'd' (Dog). The change is deliberate because the poet wants to contrast the 'planting of the corpse' by Stetson in the modern wasteland with the ritual planting of the corpse in Christianity and pre-Christian religions, in which the Dog played the fruitful role of redemption and regeneration, the rebirth of the dead, buried under ground. The Christian idea is expressed in St. Paul's emphatic pronouncement in the *Romans:* 'know ye not that so many of us as were baptized into Jesus Christ were baptized into his death ? We are buried with him............into death.........if we have been planted together in the likeness of his death, we shall be also in the likeness of his resurrection'. This is Christian planting of the corpse which sprouted into a new life. The function of the dog in Christian devotion is elaborated in Thompson's *The Hound of Heaven* where God. like a hound, pursues the soul, flying into the arms of spiritual death and brings about its final redemption. This Christian idea was enacted in the old fertility rituals, connected with the death and resurrection of the vegetation gods. In Egypt, for example, the corpse of Osiris, the fertility god, was first dismembered, but later the scattered limbs were collected by his beloved, Isis, with the aid of dogs. Then, there may be a reference to the Dog Star, Sirius, rising in the hottest part of the dry season and heralding the rise of the Nile water and return of fertility to the barren soil, and hope of life to the parched and thirsty vegetation. Lastly, reference has been made to the wish of the Cumean Sybil in *Satyricon* that a dog should be tied to her statue after her death so that she may 'attain to life after death'. This is the ritualistic side of the question related to the past ages of faith and spirituality when the burial of the dead was sure to be followed by rebirth and the dog was noted for its capacity to further this creative process.

But all this has been reversed in the wasteland wherc the planting of the corpse is literal rather than ritualistic so that its growth in a new life is problematical. All of us are sowing and planting every day but are not confident about the crop. The new plant may be bitten by frost or blasted by the cold wind. Shelley describes the function of the wild westwind which chariots the winged seeds into the dark cavities of the earth where they lie throughout the winter as corpses in their graves till the spring wind blows her clarion and rouses them back into a new life. But it is not certain that all of them will break the spell of sleep. The Parable of the Sower in the Bible reminds us that the seeds falling on the stony soil cannot germinate, while those on the wayside are eaten away by birds. Thus, the dog also, like the elements of water and fire, has become merely destructive. It is still friendly, faithful and obedient to us, yet it is prone to scratch the ground and dig up what is buried there. So the warning is given against its destructive nail. Critics have pointed out the opposite side—i.e. the destructive implication of 'dog'—dog, as a symbol of death: 'those who sharpen the tooth of the dog that is Death. cf. the Psalmist's cry, 'Deliver my soul from the sword, my darling from the power of the Dog'. Professor Cleanth Brooks is inclined to take the 'Dog' for Humanitarianism and the allied philosophies which in their concern for man extirpate the supernatural—dig up the corpse of the buried god and thus prevent the re-birth of life. This view has been rejected by Helen Gardner in unqualified terms, but I find it quite interesting. In our commercial and godless community man has been reduced to the bare animal plane and our reformers are apt to stress the necessity of the economic and political remedies to keep man happy, as if he were framed to feed merely and his feasting alone were his happiness. Having this superficial view of man in mind Carlyle pilloried Benthamism—the greatest happiness of the greatest number—as the 'pig philosophy', a blind Samson pulling down the very structure of man's real life and seeking deliverance only in Death. The full implication of this reversal comes in the words of Gerontion, where God, the creator and sustainer, becomes a mere destroyer: 'In the juvenescence of the year came Christ, the tiger... us he devours'. This means that those who fail to imbibe life and energy from God will have to bear the brunt of His fury which may entail their total death or destruction. This is the meaning of the 'burial of the dead' in the wasteland, where there is little hope of re-birth, because 'death-wish' has overpowered Eros, the principle of life.

A Game of Chess

The second movement of the poem explores the failure of the central situation in fertility myths—namely, the relation between man and woman in love and marriage. The title, '*A Game of Chess*' introduces a complex symbol to suggest the many-sided collapse of this fundamental relationship in the wasteland with dire consequences, apt to flow from the total unawareness of the deeper spiritual meaning of sex. The first and most obvious implication of the Game lies in its association with Middleton's bitter play, *Women Beware Women* mentioned in the 'notes' to the poem. It may be given in the illuminating words of Miss Elizabeth Drew: "There (in the play) the game is used to distract the attention of a simple woman while the Duke seduces her daughter-in-law, and the seduction is described ironically in terms of the moves of the pieces on the board. The whole play, indeed, is nothing but a battle of sexual intrigue, where piece after piece falls to the manoeuvres of the opponents until finally death checkmates all"

(T. S. Eliot: *The Design of his Poetry*—p. 101).

So the first implication is the utter denial of the need of discipline in sexual relationship, turning it into a source of mere titillation or gratification of the senses at any cost. The consequence is a state of checkmate in family life. In the game of chess it is the crucial point where further movement becomes barred and the game threatens to come to an end. In the poem the idea of stalemate covers the condition in high life as well as in low life. In the first, the superficial pursuit of pleasures has resulted in an unbearable boredom—'my nerves are bad to-night', and vacuity of life, 'the greater torment of desire fulfilled', while in the low sphere opposed to it, the lack of discipline in married life—marriage as a mere device for carnal enjoyment which turns the poor wife into a premature 'hag' utterly incapable of catching the eye and engaging the heart of her roving husband. Lastly, the chessgame fitly symbolizes the prolonged but futile cerebration so characteristic of such empty souls, the exercise of the mind without direction, endless meditation upon problems which defy solution. In the first part of the section, this idea is emphasized in the broken and frenzied queries of the neurotic lady, 'what are you thinking', where the pattern is 'thinking, thinking, thinking, think'. Then comes the second series, 'Do you see nothing' etc, which gives the answering formula, 'nothing, nothing, nothing'. In the second part, the scene is the Pub, a set of women are talking about the lot of poor Lil, unmindful of the impatient cry of the waiter, 'Hurry up, please, it is time'. It means that time is fleeting put the problem facing the person and mental worry engendered by it is unending—'empty shuttles weave the wind'.

The opening lines, magnificent in their beauty and movement, visualize the drawing-room of Belladonna, the lady of Rocks, of stuations, with special emphasis upon brilliant and artistic details, each 'with its loaded intensification of sensuous opulence and prodigality' so that the eye is dazzled and sense drowned in the overpowering 'cloud of perfume'. The lines are a mosaic of quotations, significant words and phrases of other poets woven cunningly by a technique which has been aptly described as Eliot's poetic short-hand. Each phrase is a sort of verbal filament which links the lady to such grand martyrs ef unlawful love as Cleopatra of Shakespeare and Queen Dido of Virgil. Among minor references mention may be made of those which recall the description of the sleeping chamber of Imogen in Shakespeare's *Cymbeline*, a story of pretended rape of a pure and devoted wife. Imogen was stated to be reading a book before her sleep and the turned page described the story of Philomela's brutal rape, which brings that great myth also into the present perspective. Mr. Giorgio Melchiori, author of *The Tightrope Walkers*, has pointed out that the most significant connection here is Lamia (popularly known from Keats's famous poem), the serpent woman of mediaeval legend, one among the series of fatal women of decadent Romantic movement in the late nineteenth century.

This connection defines the nature of Belladonna and distinguishes her from such passionate heroines as Cleopatra and Dido. Their dignity lay in the intensity of their passion, though unlawful. Cleopatra and Antony were almost immortalized by their love—'eternity was in our lips and eyes' and even death was transfigured by their passion. The dying Cleopatra makes Death itself a passionate lover:

> The strokes of death are like the lover's pinch
> Which hurts and is yet desired.

Similarly Dido burns with a consuming passion which is quieted only by the flames of the pyre on which she immolates her tortured body and mind. But sexual love in the wasteland is a languid operation of a bored body and cloyed heart.

'The chair she sat in' recalls the famous description of Cleopatra in her barge proceeding to meet Antony. 'The chair she sat in like a burnished throne Burned on the water. The association echoes through the following lines also, which describe her glass framed in curiously carved standards wrought with fruitful vines, from which golden cupids peeped out. They were glittering with the glare of the chandelier, re-inforcing the effect of light reflected on the table. Heaps of rich jewels glittered there brilliantly and sent their own sparkle up to meet the light. Then there were open vials of ivory and glass full of perfume, cosmetics and unguents which diffused their strong scent in the air and overpowered the sense with 'too much sweet'. The current of air passing through the window stirred the scent and pushed it up like a cloud of vapour to feed and fatten the candle flames. This whole description is reminiscent of Imogen's bed-chamber, which leads to the next major association, namely, the festal Hall of Dido in Virgil's *Aeneid*, where the Queen prepared a royal reception for Aeneas, the Trojan hero. The significant words in Virgil should be noted: 'Lighted lamps hang out from the fretted ceiling (laquearia), and flaming torches drive out the night'. Here the 'prolonged candle flames' flooding the ceiling with light mingled with cloud of perfume illuminated the ornamental designs on the ceiling. Then there was her fire-place, 'framed by the coloured stone and lighted with the green and orange flame rising from the 'huge sea-wood fed with copper'. 'The carved dophin swimming in the sad light, sends our imagination back to Cleopatra's description of Antony's pleasures which were 'like dophin and showed their backs above the element'. The allusion is quite ironical in its sense of contrast. Then comes the picture of Philomel's change into the nightingale after her brutal rape by Tereus, husband of her sister, Procne—rape followed by the cutting off of her tongue.

'Yet there the nightingale filled all the desert' etc. These are crucial lines and present a favourite idea of Eliot which we have already explained in the discussion of this myth introduced in the closing lines of 'Sweeney Among the Nightingales'.

Briefly stated, Eliot's interpretation of the rape of Philomela and her change into the nightingale of 'golden voice' underlines the transforming effect of suffering willingly accepted as a fruitful spiritual discipline. Philomela thus converted her suffering and shame into the purgatorial fire, her tainted human body died and out of it the nightingale of pure and entrancing song sprang into life. The song filled the spiritual desert in antiquity and its peculiar notes 'Jug, Jug, Jug' are still heard, proclaiming, as it were, the significance of the old myth. But they are falling upon the dirty ears of the degraded worldings who take no heed and follow the beaten path of their sordid joys and mean recreations. The 'dirty ears' cannot realize the underlying wisdom of the nightingale's song. Without inner receptiveness external values are meaningless. These values are eternal but require a true response from a genuine heart to fructify in the life. Francis Thompson has rightly said:

Angels keep their ancient places,
Turn but a stone and start a wing.

But our visions are now changed and we are not able to see them. One is reminded of the significant lines of Shakespeare in the final Act of *The Merchant of Venice,* which refer to the music of spheres and then tell us that there is identical music in the soul of man also but so long as we are encased in our 'muddy vesture of decay' we are not even conscious of it. We have said elsewhere that wisdom is not a gift but an acquisition; even when it descends like grace from heaven to the place beneath, its effect is felt only in a state of inner purification and illumination. Browning has shown the truth of this fact in the beautiful song of Pippa which proves a turning-point in the lives of several characters facing a crisis.

It is no wonder that the myth of Philomela and other legends painted on the walls of this luxury room have become mere 'withered stumps', relics of the dead past now shorn of their meaning, used merely to decorate the room, not to order our life. 'As though a window gave upon the sylvan scene', links the scene with Milton's Eden where Eve, prototype of all womanhood, was successfully tempted and degraded by Satan. This is another reminder of the old concept of sin, followed by suffering which should be accepted as a penance for the purgation of sin and purification of the soul. That this is a basic idea of Eliot is borne out by a number of his remarks in his criticism as well as his creative writings: Poetry 'can find its material only in suffering'; the struggle which actually makes the poet 'is the struggle to transmute his personal and private agonies into something rich and strange, something universal and impersonal'. 'Hell and purgatory', says Miss Elizabeth Drew, "are familiar territories to him; release from them fleeting and infrequent, is won only by unrelenting self-discipline, 'a training of the soul as severe and ascetic as the training of the body of a runner'; the comfort in the pain only that 'the souls in purgatory suffer because they wish to suffer, for purgation".

(T. S. Eliot: *The Design of His Poetry*, p. 52)

The same critic has drawn our attention to the explosive effect of the word '*synthetic*' in the description—her strange *synthetic* perfume—which forcibly reminds us that the splendour of this lady is not natural and genuine but artificial and tawdry like her inner self. The point receives great emphasis in the actual description of the woman doing her hair under the blaze of light in a state of nervous excitement, caused by the impending visit of her lover. 'Her hair glowed into words and then would be savagely still'. The lines bring to mind Swinburne's famous description of a fatal woman in a celebrated Italian drawing. Here also 'the electric hair which looks as though it would hiss and glitter with spark, if once touched'. This associates the lady with Lamia and other fatal women. The association is further emphasized by the clear reminiscence of Dante's hell-flame, the tip of which 'would move and glow into words'. The lady, thus, is viewed as a modern version of the cruel beauties whose kiss was fatal, but now she is in the decay of her vigour—a defunct dragon—paralysed within, the heart gone dry, the nerves shattered to bits—a neurotic woman crushed under the burden of her monotonous life.

This psychological breakdown is powerfully expressed in the cryptic, excited and almost hectic colloquy which ensues:

> My nerves are bad to night etc.
> What are you thinking of? What thinking?
> What?
> I never know what you are thinking. Think.

The answer repeats 'nothin, nothing, nothing'. A sad comment upon their mental emptiness ! The echoes of Webster, Shakespeare's *Hamlet* and *Macbeth* from 'What is that noise?'

> The wind under the door. etc.

to 'Is there nothin in your head?' enrich the association of guilt and nervous breakdown. This barren mental agitation and sense of imprisonment in a life of dead monotony and crushing narrowness remind us of the Hollow Men:

> Head piece filled with straw
> Our dried voices when we whisper together
> Are quiet and meaningless

As wind in dry grass
Or rats' feet over broken glass
    In our dry cellar.

Here also the silent interlocutor opens his lips only to say—

I think we are in rats' alley
Where the dead men lost their bones.

Again he remarks:

I remember
Those are pearls that were his eyes.

The significant lines from Shakespeare's *Tempest* with their emphasis on the transforming power of water and the process of re-birth out of the very heart of death are remembered mechanically as a meaningless formula. Under further pressure from the lady's nervous tongue: 'Are you alive, or not? Is there nothing in your head'? he gives out a sudden but constrained ejaculation like a spurt of soda-water from the bottle:

0, 0, 0, that Shakespearean Rag
It's so elegant so intelligent

Thus the noble fragment of poetry with its deep spiritual meaning has become only a bit of 'rag rhyme', sound without sense. Meanwhile the nervousness of the lady is mounting and she is even thinking desperately to cast all formalities to the four winds and throw off the chains which have fixed her cruelly in her narrow cage: 'I shall rush out as I am, and walk the street' etc. The recurring patterns of monotonous and dead routine of daily life are unbearable to recall:

> The hot water at ten.
> And if it rains, a closed car at four.
> And we shall play a game of chess,
> Pressing lidless eyes and waiting for a knock upon the door.

The game of chess becomes the symbol of this empty life when the mind is exercised on petty considerations and the eyes are fixed languidly and helplessly on the move and counter-move of the game, intellectual as well as sexual, and the weary heart waits for some violence which may knock this life to pieces or death itself which may put an end to this stale and aimless existence. But this weary waiting has no hope.

'We also wait but not like thee in hope', as Arnold feelingly puts it. This is a poignant picture of stalemate in high-life which has come to a dead end, a life without any positive aim or serious business;

> What shall I do now ? What shall I do
> What shall we do tomorrow ? What shall we ever do.

This stalemate throws back a revealing flood of light on the otherwise obscure lines towards the close of the grand description which introduces the lady:

> Staring forms
> Leaned out, leaning, hushing the room enclosed.

Apparently the lines refer to the pictures on the walls etc., which silently stared at the articles in the room, deepening the effect of silence. We are reminded of the carved angels in Keats's *Eve of St.*

Agnes, which gazed all the while on the scene below. But in Keats the scene is one of great excitement and exhilaration and though the heroine is the very picture of fixity in that storm, her heart is quite voluble with emotion. But here the silence in the enclosed room is a symbol of the deadness of the whole existence to which the lady is tied.

The scene shifts to the pub., where the stalemate of married life is described in a conversation among a set of women reprsenting lower stratum of society. It is a deceitful friend of a poor and hard-pressed woman, Lil by name, who is giving an account of her collapsed marriage-relationship. Lil has lost her youth prematurely under the strain of child-bearing and the pills she had to take for dissolving the last conception has rendered her 'antique' and almost toothless. But her husband, just returned from service abroad, wants her to be smart and attractive to keep him from going to more engaging women for 'having a good time'. Marriage means children and in children the mother is reborn but the young wife dies. The qualities of motherhood are different from those of an attractive young wife and a husband should have the wisdom to realize the fact. In the absence of such a wisdom and self-restraint marriage will be a burden and curse upon the poor woman. Here we are provided with a 'knocking at the gate'—Hurry up please it's time—the peremptory words of the keeper who wants to close the pub. But the knock is not heeded because the problem of life defies all attempt at solution within limits of time. The problem is long though time is fleeting. The closing line of the section 'Goodnight ladies etc'. echoes the words of Ophelia, a poor, innocent but spineless girl who fell an easy victim to the cruelty of her lover. Through her the fate of helpless Lil receives an added significance and poignancy, despite all apparent contrasts in their external conditions.

THE FIRE SERMON

The title of the section is derived from the famous sermon preached by the Buddha to the assembled priests on the pain arising from the reckless pursuit of the desires of the senses. The whole world is on fire, burning 'with the fire of passion, with the fire of hatred, with the fire of infatuation; with birth, old age, death, sorrow, lamentation, misery, grief and despair are they on fire'. This view of the human life lived purely on the sensual plane is supported by the words of St Augustine, a true representative of asceticism in Christianity. His confessions refer to his youthful temptations: 'To Carthage then I came, where a cauldron of unholy love sang all about my ears'. 'I also entangle my steps in the outward beauties: but thou wilt pluck me out, O Lord, thou wilt pluck me out'. The collocation of these two representatives of eastern and western asceticism, Eliot has reminded us, is not an accident. It means that the intention here is to present life in the wasteland as a reckless surrender to the senses and all the abnormality, morbidity and perversion to which they lead, though wise teachers have every-where preached the necessity of control and continence to escape their burning effect. This shows a total breakdown of the old discipline in the modern world which has understood only one side of Freud's sex-psychology and paid little heed to his warning against the 'night side' of the human ego.

The section begins with a dreary autumn scene on Thames-side and glances at the contamination of the river water by the commercial and sexual mud of our day. The wanton disregard for the purity of a river which is the life-line cf England symbolizes the poisoning of the moral and sexual life of the people at its very source. Behind this dirty Thames we are kept constantly aware of the presence of Spenser's 'Sweet Thames' as described in his '*Prothalamion*'. In Spenser the significant details are the purity of the river's water, the beauty of the banks bedecked with flowers, with young ladies in immaculate attire picking flowers to make garlands against 'the mariage day which is not long', while the bride-grooms are introduced as a pair of swans floating on the limpid surface of the river, with feathers so spotlessly white, indeed, that even the pure water appears to be a threat to their whiteness. But now even the shady trees which formed a tent of foliage over the river have become bare and the last lingering leaves are dropping slowly, in the mud, trying all through their downward passage along the branches to catch at them, as it were, with eager fingers. The wind passes through the bare branches with no rustling sound; the landscape is wrapped in a brown fog and the nymphs (old as well as new) are no more to be seen. In the summer season the bank was haunted by batches of merry-makers and chance lovers who wasted a good many hours in eating, drinking, talking, laughing, 'ogling and all that' as Pope happily puts it. The river bore testimony to their orgies in the shape of empty bottles, silk-handkerchiefs and cigarette-ends etc., which mingled with its water and drifted along its currents. The modern nymphs, however, are different from those of Spenser; they are the lighthearted, often poor, pleasure-hungry girls who frequent the banks of the river to meet the young sons and heirs of rich London merchants, with easy money and no work to do, in order to give them a good time and complete their recreational programmes. But now these chance lovers are no where to be seen and they may not meet each other again because their encounter was for a moment's recreation only, which becomes stale if repeated with the same partner. So they have left no addresses. The protagonist is thus left alone to watch the scene and lament its decay.

The protagonist's lamentation by the waters of the Thames brings to mind other such lamentations in history and literature which charge the present scene with serious implications and make the pollution of the river-water an alarming symptom. As Tiresias is the symbol of human consciousness, who has fore-suffered all, so he can very well relate those lamentations as if they were all his personal experiences.

'By the waters of Leman I sat down and wept'. Here the poet has telescoped two familiar incidents—the captive Jews weeping 'by the rivers of Babylon' for their motherland, and Bonnivard in Byron's *Prisoner of Chillon* pining in captivity below the bed of Lake Leman for light and freedom. Other memories and sensations crowd into his mind as he sits, like a member of the modern community in the wasteland, fishing in the dull canal behind the gas-house, swept by the cold wind which brings to his ear the noisc, the chatter and 'the chuckle spread from ear to ear' i. e. the hearty but fatuous laughter of the men and women who are like skeletons rattling in the wind. The allusion to Marvell's poem—*To His Coy Mistress*—brings the ironic contrast home to us:

> But ever at my back I hear
> Time's winged chariot, hurrying near;
> And yonder all before us lie
> Deserts of vast eternity.

But the modern desert is one of death—the desert full of bones, the picture of 'evil land' in the Bible; and the fishing is only literal, catching fish for dinner amid dirty surroundings—'a rat crept softly through the vegetation, dragging its slimy belly'. The symbolical meaning of fishing and water—fertility and transformation into something rich and strange–is enforced by the later allusion to the brother of the Fisher King, lamenting the impotency of the King and fishing for his re-birth, and secondly, to Prince Ferdinand in Shakespere's *Tempest*, who sat by the sea to weep for his drowned father, little knowing and so needing a reminder from Ariel, that drowning is a medium of rebirth and water a life-giving and transforming element. But in the wasteland water also is a destructive element as is witnessed by the naked dead bodies floating on the river-surface:

> White bodies naked on the low damp ground
> And bones cast in a little low dry garret
> Rattled by the rat's foot only, year to year.

We have met with this image of modern life in the previous section—'We are in rat's alley where dead men lost their bones'. This is the picture of the humdrum, monotonous treadmill of purely animal existence moving in a vicious circle— a universe of death where men and women are mere ghosts, where 'no contact of sense can allay the fever of the bones' as Eliot says in the Donne passage quoted in the first section.

This completes the general outline of the scene, the sordid details of which occupy the rest of this section.

At the back of the protagonist comes the sound of horns etc. which at once recalls the lines in John Day's *Parliament of Bees* (1607):

> 'When of the sudden, listening, you shall hear,
> A noise of horns and hunting, which shall bring
> Actaeon to Diana in the spring,
> Where all shall see her naked skin.

It is the story of a daring mortal, Actaeon, the Greek hunter, chancing to cast his eye upon the naked beauty of bathing Diana, goddess of chastity and at once suffering the penalty for his accidental stupidity......... which was, his sudden change into a stag on which his own hounds fell with fury and ravenous hunger, tearing their own master to pieces. The old picture of terrible chastity and holy bathing clashes sharply with its modern and degraded counterpart. Here the sound is the horn of the car which is to bring Mr. Sweeney, a vulgar lump of our industrial society, frankly given to carnal pleasures, to Mrs. Porter, modern 'Diana', short of all vestiges of chastity, who along with her daughter washes her feet in soda-water to catch more flies in her lustful web. It is a travesty at once of the bathing of Diana in her sacred pool and the ritual washing of the body or feet in religious rites, as a process preparatory to and symptomatic of the inner purification. Nothing can show the cheapness and meanness of our modern way of life more sharply than 'soda-water'. This picture of the vulgarization of something which once was holy and spiritual is supported by two more references which follow. The French quotation *Et O ccs*—'O those children's voices, singing in the choir'—is taken from Verlain's *Parsifal* which presents the quest of Grail from our modern, vulgar point of view. Here the hero, Parsifal, comes within the hearing of the sweet voices of children singing in the Grail temple, but their sound does not bring joy and holy calm to him as it did to his prototype in antiquity. It, on the contrary, thrills his homosexual instinct and he is of a mind to debauch the innocents. This is followed by the sound of the nightingale with its characteristic significance to the dirty ears of modern vulgarians..........'so rudely foreed—Tereu'. It is not the 'inviolable' beauty of the song born out of suffering which the modern ear can find here, but simply and solely, the idea of rape which the story seems to convey as an eternal sanction for man's brutality to helpless women and also to young boys. Eliot has in mind the numerous Elizabethan references to the song of the nightingale and its mythical association. Here is one from Lyly:

> What bird so sings, yet so does wail ?
> O ! it is the ravished nightingale.
> Jug, Jug, Jug, Tereu, she cries,
> And still her woes at midnight rise.

The story of the nightingale thus becomes a symbol of the woeful tales of all helpless young women who are crushed under the brutal assaults of men. Eliot later introduces modern specimens of this class.

But what immediately engages our attention is the suggestion of what Milton has called 'the worse rape', the unnatural intercourse between man and man. The irony of the fact lies in making the 'Smyrna Merchant (the one-eyed merchant) the plague-spot in this matter. Miss Weston has pointed out that the Syrian merchants were the main carriers of the fertility cult to Europe, that commerce and religion were like their two eyes, and they set up their temple and their counting-house side by side. But now the eye of religion is blasted and they carry only articles of merchandise and the worse freight of homosexuality. So Mr. Eugenides, the Smyrna merchant unshaven, comes to the 'unreal city', wrapped in the brown winter-fog, with his pockets full of currants (dry merchandise) and the Bill of Lading, 'carriage and insurance free' to London, and invites the protagonist in slangy French to lunch at the Cannon Street hotel to be followed by a weekend holiday at the Metropole. The meaning of the insidious invitation becomes clear when we remember that both the hotels were notorious for assignations and homosexual debauch, more particularly during the years following the end of the first world war.

This is followed by the equally sordid mating of the female typist with her 'young man carbuncular'. The female typist is a human machine tied to the pitiless drudgery of the desk. She works all the day like an 'engine' but at the end of the day she raises her eyes and back from her mechanical work and is filled with a longing for release and for her return home. Her mechanical heart begins to throb and she sits waiting for the hour which will give her a respite from her killing job. 'Like a taxi throbbing waiting' is an instance of an ordinary urban image raised to the height of poetic intensity and suggestiveness. Tiresias, though blind, can fully visualize the scene of the evening, 'the violet hour' and understand its meaning in relation to women like the female typist, who have nothing human left in them after their day's work. He has experienced life both as male and female and the marks of bisexuality are writ large on his person.........he is 'an old man with wrinkled female breasts.' The evening home-coming of the typist raises many associations in his mind, which are concentrated in a single phrase.........'the evening hour that brings the sailor from the sea'. It is reminiscent of Sappho's beautiful lines to the evening star, 'Hesperus, you bring all that the bright morning scattered, the sheep, the kid, and the child to its mother'. It may also remind us of Stevenson's *Requiem:* 'Home is the sailor home from the sea'. These echoes cast a melancholy light on the home-coming of the typist, who is moving from active boredom to passive dullness of a lonely existence. The description of her room is intended to stress her poverty and hardship—her food is in tin-pots and out of her window are hanging perilously not the magic garments of Prospero, but the washed clothes of a poor woman, while her divan, her sole bed at night, is now littered with the articles of her dress. After tea she feels momentarily refreshed and is psychologically conditioned for the amorous encounter with her young man, which, however, is neither passionately anticipated nor heartily reciprocated.

Tiresias, in this context, has drawn our pointed attention to his androgynous nature and his experience of life, for seven years, as a woman. Later on in lines beginnig with 'I, Tiresias, have foresuffered all', he makes it perfectly clear that his experiences were mostly those of poor women like the typist here who are generally bored and tired of their daily labour, very hard and unpleasant, so that in moments of brief relaxation and comparative leisure their moral fibres are loosened and their power of resisting the frank overtures and bold assaults of a sex-intoxicated lover is reduced to the minimum. On such occasions, therefore, the unscrupulous man may play with their persons even though they themselves remain throughout only indifferent and passive agents. Eliot has quoted a long Latin passage from Ovid's *Metamorphoses* where the whole history of Tiresias' peculiar nature and gift is contained in a nut-shell. It says how this man of Thebes once chanced upon a pair of huge serpents mating in a forest and how he outraged them with a blow of his staff and underwent a miraculous change of his person into that of a woman which lasted for seven years. In the eighth year, however, he came across the same serpents in identical situation and struck them again to find himself back into his original male form. Because of his strange position as a Hermaphrodite he was approached to arbitrate in a dispute between god Jove and his imperious consort, Juno, who were divided over the interesting question whether the man or the woman is more prone to the pleasures of love, each blaming the other sex. Tiresias sided with the male disputant, Jove, and declared the woman as the more eager party in the amorous sports. Juno was infuriated and cursed the judge to be blind for good and all. Jove, however, matched this curse with his indemnifying boon, the gift of prophecy, power to penetrate into the mysteries of the present and the future. Tiresias, thus, is best fitted for the role which Eliot has assigned to him in the present poem, which is otherwise devoid of plot and hero.

The 'expected guest' is introduced as a 'young man carbuncular', with a bold stare in his eyes, a person of low means, a poor house-agent's clerk, in whom boldness is not a natural trait but an occasional mask which has to be assumed deliberately and even then it may look unnatural. Boldness is a natural property of the fortunate life and high station where the right to command and overawe the persons of lower rank is almost a birth-right. Eliot compares the uneasy 'assurance' of this person to the 'silk hat on Bradford Millionaire', the comparison is as startling as it is pregnant and effective and thus capable of providing a lasting satisfaction to perceptive readers. The poet is referring to a class of businessmen in London who had grown rich overnight during the war and were thus in a position to dress and live decently like men of wealth and good breeding. But cultivated manners can not be picked up in a day or two because culture is a thing of slow growth and unless a person inherits it as a precious legacy and is born in it he is bound to remain a mere ape of fashion even in his dress and external mode of life. A person may purchase a costly silk hat but his money will not give him the capacity to feel easy under it. In this way 'the silk hat' remains a mere external decoration under which the head is uneasy. But the 'bold' young man is shrewd enough to realize the fitness of the occasion to have his way with a woman who is bored and tired after her mechanical work and is least disposed to resist his attempt. So he at once sets to work, gingerly touching and caressing the various parts of her body, encouraged by her passivity and making a virtue of her indifference, which, in his vanity, he takes to be her consent. So the thing is done and the gratified man is not inclined to waste any more time in unnecessary conversation with his silent partner and giving her a parting and 'patronising kiss' he at once beats, if not a hasty, at least a silent and cautious retreat down the dark stair-case. Tiresias, who has 'walked among the lowest of the dead and sat by the Thebes below the wall', perhaps among the beggars, comments that the affair between the typist and the 'young man carbuncular', is by no means a stray fact in an individual life, but a representative experience shared by poor women in all ages, when work becomes a drudgery and life an unrelieved repetition of inanities. After the silent departure of her bold but heartless lover, the typist consults her mirror to make sure that no damage has been done to her face and complexion, mentally relieved that the business, good, bad or indifferent, is at last over. So she moves about in the room and her hand mechanically passes to her head to smooth her hair. The ironical comment of the poet comes with a sharp reminder of a different 'lovely woman who stooped to folly' as described in a wel-known song in Goldsmith's *The Vicar of Wakefield:*

> When lovely woman stoops to folly,
> And finds too late that men betray,
> What charm can soothe her melancholy ?

What art can wash her guilt away ?
The only art her guilt to cover
To hide her shame from every eye,
To give repentance to her lover
And wring his bosom—is to die.'

Eliot is referring to a strong moral attitude towards sexual relationship where violation of her chastity for a betrayed woman is worse than death and makes further existence impossible. But in the case of the typist and women of the type in the wasteland, sex itself has become a mechanical operation, a mere coupling of animals, involving no sense of good or evil. The mechanical nature of this business is emphasized by such words as 'automatic hand' and 'record on a gramophone'. The consummmate handlng of anti-climax in the passage is too obvious to need any explanation.

Following this mechanical music, like Ferdinand under the spell of the song of Ariel, the protagonist moves along the Strand, up Queen Victoria Street, towards the lower reaches of the Thames where the sailors live a communal life in the real sense of the term, as has been noted by other observers also. The ears of the protagonist are greeted by the pleasant note of a mandoline and the human sound of talk and laughter mingled with the clatter of plying spoons in the hotel where fishermen are gathered together to relax and refresh themselvest at noon. In the heart of this community there stands the Church, St. Magnus Martyr, with its beautiful interior of 'Ionian white and gold' with their unspeakable splendour. Eliot has noted: 'The interior of St. Magnus Martyr is to my mind one of the finest among Wren's interiors'. But even this area is not free from the sexual stain which the inhabitants of the wasteland communicate, with their vulgar contact with the life of the poor people, who have at least the sense to realize the tragedy involved in the loss of female purity and chastity. This idea is the inspiring motive behind the songs of the Thames-daughters which follow. These are the poor girls of this area, victims of the thoughtless lust of vulgar men, who are lamenting at once the loss of their virginity and the equally tragic loss of the river's purity, which, in a way, symbolizes the universal dirtiness peculiar to the human life in the modern wasteland. The section is based upon two of the famous operas of Wagner, *Das Rheingold* and *Gotter dammerung*, where three Rhine-daughters first sing of the gold in the river which they guard and then, in the second, mourn its loss which implies the loss of the purity of river water. The refrain is taken from the first.

The first song, 'The river sweats', presents a vivid picture of the river surface oozing with the mud of modern commerce. The style is a fine specimen of imagism where each word is concrete and pictorial. The water of the river becomes a living body 'sweating oil and tar'. One is reminded of Masefield's *Cargoes* which emphasizes the cheap and dirty nature of modern commodities as distinguished from the precious and beautiful articles which ships in olden days used to bring to their countries. 'Barges drift, red sail, wide' presents the whole picture of the pleasure boats, with red sails on, drifting down the tide, splashing water on the logs floating down Greenwich reach etc.

In the second scene we are given a glimpse of the past; the royal pleasure-trip of Elizabeth and her lover-for the nonce—the earl of Leicester. It is a royal barge of great splendour with its stern of 'gilded shell' of red and gold colour, sweeping briskly under the favourable force of the south-west wind. Critics have drawn our attention to the historic significance of the typical pleasure-trip of Queen Elizabeth I, with her lover, Lord Robert, with whom she, at times, became so familiar that the observers wondered why she should not marry the man apparently so near her heart, yet the Queen remained the virgin queen of England. It has been pointed out that the splendour of the Queen is only in apparent contrast with the squalor of the modern Thames and her humble daughters because the royal love-making is essentially identical with that which the poor girls are lamenting, and the argument is supported by Eliot's own remark that all women are one woman. Yet, I feel that there is a crucial contrast between the two sterile loves. In the case of the Elizabeth-Leicester episode the superiority lies with the woman who can play the game of love to her heart's content and keep her virginity intact in the sequel. But the Thames-daughters are the victims of the superior male force and their momentary weakness proves fatal to their honour. What the episode is epecially pointing at is the suppression of the feminine element in the modern civilization which is all-male in its swagger and brutality. All the examples of sterile love in this section bear witness to the violence of the male partners and the utter passivity and helplessness of the females.

The main theme is introduced by the third song, 'Trams and dusty trees' where the singer regretfully glances at her fall. 'Highbury bore me', etc. is reminiscent of Pia's remark in Dante's *Purgatorio:* 'Remember me, who am Pia. Siena made me, Maremma unmade me' and also of Virgil's epitaph, 'Matua bore me, Calabria was the death of me, now Naples holds me'. Richmond and Kew are riverside vacation-stops haunted by pleasure-seekers and one of such visitors ruined the girl in a country boat. The stanzas which follow seem to be the continuation of the same story but they may as well be sung by her companions because the fates of all the three are identical.

'My feet are at Moorgate' etc. This is the picture of the girl after the shameful event with its memory rankling in her heart. She is walking the street in the heart of London where she is perhaps an employee, but her heart is in a state of abject humiliation (under her shoes, as it were). She remembers that her ravisher was repentant after the event and promised to turn over a new leaf, to which her silence was the only comment, even her anger was out of place because it was quite impotent. 'On Margate Sand' repeats the story of the fall of a helpless girl in a sea-side resort near London. The girl realizes the utter emptiness of her life, the connection of her present and her past is meaningless like the addition of one zero to another. The utter degradation and futility of the poor life is powerfully expressed by an apparently trite image which likens her life to a dirty hand of which the past and the present are like broken finger-nails which cannot be joined together. And the heart of this nothingness lies in 'my people humble people who expect nothing', the utter helplessness of the humble, honest people who can only suffer, like dumb animals, all the wrongs which the powerful brutes heap on them. The section closes with the words of the Buddha, 'burning, burning, burning', supported by the confessions of St. Augustine 'to Carthage then I came' which we have quoted at lenght at the opening of our discussion of this part of the poem. The poet intends to emphasize the supreme necessity of moral discipline and continence which the wisdom of the East and the West is at one in inculcating as the one way of escaping the flames of lust and desire which are constantly threatening the human race with spiritual extinction. Fire will be extinguished if there is no supply of fuel to feed its flames.

Death by Water

The fourth movement make a transition from the burning flames to water of the ocean or, it may be, the river which, we expect, can offer a relief from the heat of the fire and effectually wash away all the stains of the body as well as of the soul. The expectation is apparently supported by the stately, slow-moving rhythm with its gentle rise and fall, creating the impression of the undulating waves advancing to embrace in their cooling arms:

Phlebas the Phoenician, a fortnight dead
Forgot the cry of gulls, and the deep sea swell
And the profit and loss.

But a momentary glance at the lines dashes that hope down and rudely reminds us that in this wasteland, water, too, has become as destructive as fire and instead of the creation of a new life through the transformation of the old one ('those are pearls that were his eyes'), it simply swallows up a man, young, handsome and physically strong. The drowned Phoenician sailor described here is his own cousin to the one-eyed Smyrna merchant in the third section, a type of vulgar trader thinking only of his profit and loss and the cry of seagulls, i. e. sensuous pleasures and recreations. His life was simply a circular movement round profit, loss and pleasures; and when after death his bones are caught by the current they simply repeat the same circular process in a direction reverse to the rhythm of his life. Life is a round of birth, growth, maturity, age and death, and after death the opposite process starts—age, youth and childhood, and ultimately total oblivion into the whirlpool of water. The warning, to Gentile or Jew, so clearly reminiscent of the words of St. Paul in *Romans* 3: 9: '...... We have before proved both Jews and Gentiles, that they are all under sin', brings the idea home to us that the case of this merchant, who was once so handsome and tall, has a lesson for all persons, irrespective of race and religion, who have to steer their ships and watch the wind in course of their voyage on the ocean. It means that all of us are voyagers on the sea of life where we have to pass through the temptations of wealth and of the senses, and if we suffer ourselves to be overborne by those temptations our life will be only a whirling wheel followed by the vortex of death. This is the wheel of worldly existence which becomes a key symbol in Eliot's later poetry and is contrasted with 'the still point' :

> not in movement
> But abstention from movement, while the world moves
> In appetency, on its metalled ways
> Of time past and time future.

Eliot may have been acquainted with a basic conception in Indian philosophy, quite familiar to W. B. Yeats, that the sense-ridden soul is tied to the cycle of birth, death and re-birth through endless ages till it is disciplined and enlightened by subduing the strong pull of the senses, which paves the way for its final release.

The drowning of the sailor, finally, reminds us of the sacrificial drowning of the vegetation god which was followed by his re-birth. The effigy of the god was immersed in water at Alexandria and was caught by the current, and as it rose and fell it passed through the stages of age, manhood and youth and finally did not disappear in the whirlpool but emerged into light and new-life to the tunes of the song celebrating the re-birth of the drowned god. The reference to Ariel's song in the *Tempest* that the parts of the drowned king have 'suffered a sea-change into something rich and strange' is quite obvious and pertinent to recall. In this way one more symbol of life has become a medium of death in our spiritually barren age.

What the Thunder Said

The final and perhaps the most complex and philosophical movement of the poem shows the way of release from the spiritual death, as was discovered by the hoary wisdom of India, and proclaimed to humanity by Prajapati speaking in thunder. This is indicated by the title, 'What the Thunder Said', and we shall have occasion to expatiate upon it at a later stage. The first part of the movement is taken up by three themes, as Eliot has reminded us in his notes: the mythical journey of the Knight through the thirsty land of the Fisher King to the Chapel Perilous; the biblical journey of the wavering disciples of dead Christ to Emmaus, which ended in the revelation of the mystery of Resurrection; and the aimless journey of the uprooted modern humanity through the regions of the fertility cult in Eastern Europe, which is on the brink of total collapse, the once homogeneous society breaking to fragments.

The opening lines describe the scene of Christ's arrest by the crowd headed by his betrayer, Judas: 'Judas, then, having received a band of men and officers from the chief priests and Pharisees, cometh thither with lanterns and torches and weapons'. 'Torchlight red' in the first line conveys the sense of terror and violence. 'Frosty silence in the gardens' refers to death-like silence which prevailed in the garden of Gethsemane after Christ had been taken away by the noisy crowd. 'Gardens' implies that the story of Christ's death typifies the stories of all the hanged, drowned and buried fertility gods described by Frazer in his *Golden Bough.* 'Agony in stony places' refers to the suffering of Christ in the prison at the hands of the hostile officers and functionaries. 'Shouting and crying' etc. refers to the noisy demonstration of Christ's enemies before the prison and also before the palace of Pilate, the Roman governor, against the proposed pardon and release of Christ.

'Reverberations of thunder' etc. brings the story to its final phase, namely, the hour of his agony and passion which was reflected in the convulsion and distemper of nature at the moment. Upto this time the account has moved steadily from point to point to the eve of Crusifixion, when all of a sudden it takes a surprising turn:

> 'He who was living is now dead'.

We are abruptly forced to realize the fact that the crucifixion of Christ was really a new life and new birth for him. Christ, the man, died and Christ, the god, Saviour and fountain-head of a new religion, Christianity, was re-born. Christ was not killed by his enemies, but has now been killed by the modern followers of his creed, who have forsaken him not for other gods, but for no god. The death of god, who is the fountain of living strength for man, has resulted in the process of the spiritual death of modern humanity, which, however, is so totally devoid of any spiritual sense that it does not feel even a fraction of that agony which even the son of God experienced in the fatal hour. So we are dying with a little patience and going the way of death not with a 'bang', but 'with a 'whimper' as the Hollow Men realize it.

'Here is no water but only rock'—this is the beginning of the mythical journey of Perceival and his fellow questers to the Chapel Perilous in the Fisher King's drought-ridden dominion prior to the advent of the long-awaited showers to the thirsty land, betokening the return of fertility to the sterile soil, which in its turn will reflect and follow, as a sequel, the restoration of the maimed King to his original potency and manliness. The hardships of the journey are catalogued at length and the feeling of the marchers is significantly conveyed in the haunting rhythm of the lines. The brave band is conscious all the while of the universe of rock and sand without a trace of water to allay its thirst which has parched the throats of men, as it were, with fever heat. There are wide gaps in the rocks like the mouth of old men, showing the rotten remnants of their teeth, and tawny patches of dry grass with the wind whistling menacingly through the hard and dry stalks. The song of the desert insects is unpleasant and at times the voices of ghostly figures and evil spirits, 'red sullen faces' not only strike terror but, more disconcertingly still, clearly mock at the whole undertaking as if it were really a vain pursuit of a mirage. In this way the landscape of the opening section—'what are the roots that clutch ?' etc. has been extended and more elaborately defined here, with greater awareness of the necessity of water without which life is becoming impossible.

Yes the journey is symoblical also and points to the unbearable purgatory through which the soul must pass before it is able to reach the end of its spiritual quest. It is significant also that the journey is uphill and the Chapel is situated at the peak of the mountain, which is as it should be because Truth, as Donne says, always sits on the top of the crag. F. R. Leavis has rightly pointed out that the cry 'water, water' and the frantic but futile search which is implicit in the cry clearly acquire a religious significance. It is a common idea, emphasized again and again by Eliot also, that the most important requisite for spiritual regeneration is the awareness of one's meaningless existence merely on the animal plane and intense longing for release which is best symbolized by a fierce longing for that 'water' which alone can slake the thirst of the Soul:

For the thirst that from the soul doth rise
Doth need a drink divine.

The urgency of this longing for the redeeming draught of water which alone is calculated to allay the fever of the soul is fitly conveyed in these lines:

If there were water
And no rock
....
If there were rock
And also water
If there were the sound of water only
...........Water over a rock
Where the hermit-thrush sings in the pine trees
Drip drop drip drop drop drop drop
But there is no water.

Eliot's note reminds us of the 'cool liquid water-dripping song' of the hermit-thrush. Birds in his later poetry are generally assigned a helpful role in spiritual meditation and discipline.

> There is not even solitude in the mountains
> But red sullen faces sneer and snarl
> From doors of mud-cracked houses.

Here we have a reference to a crucial experience in the process of spiritual discipline. As the soul begins to rise above the senses and the ordinary desires and attachments to life it is assailed by a strong temptation. In the life of the Buddha it is symbolized by the host of evil spirits which for several days and nights laid siege to his mind, and the same is the case with all saintly initiates. In the Grail quest the most trying experience is connected with the doubt about the reality of the object itself which has involved so much labour and pain. In the life of Christ also such a moment came during his stay in the wilderness and his experience became the type of all such experiences in less privileged mortals:

> The Word in the desert
> Is most attacked by voices of temptation
> The crying shadow in the funeral dance,
> The loud lament of disconsolate chimera,

The following lines refer to another such experience in a biblical journey, which may also be taken as a symbol of the progress of the soul from a state of doubt and uncertainty to one of full belief and faith. After the Crucifixion of Christ some of his own disciples were doubtful about his resurrection.

Once it so happened that two of such doubting Thomases were journeying to a place known as Emmaus when they became aware of a third figure walking by their side; but when they turned to look at him the vision disappeared. Eliot has drawn attention to such an illusion connected with an Antarctic expedition. But that is not material, what is important to note here is the fact that the figure of resurrected Christ appears at first as a mocking vision:

> Gliding wrapt in a brown mantle, hooded
> I do not know whether a man or woman
> But who is that on the other side of you ?

It is only in the final stage that Christ appears in person before them and sets their wavering at rest.

These two are the fruitful journeys which had definite goals, ultimately realized, though after much trial and tribulation. Eliot now proceeds to introduce the third journey—the march of uprooted humanity in the modern wasteland wandering aimlessly amid the wrecks and splitting explosions of the Christian Society, especially in Eastern Europe, the early home of the fertility cult in the western hemisphere. Eliot is drawing upon the vivid descriptions in a contemporary German work, *Blick ins Chaos* or (*On The Brink of Chaos*) by Hermann Hesse: "Already half of Europe, at least half of Eastern Europe, is on the way to chaos, travelling drunken in holy illusion, along the edge of abyss, and as she goes, sings drunken hymns······Over these songs the outraged burgher laughs scornfully, the saint and seer hears them with tears".

What is that sound high in the air
Murmur of maternal lamentation etc.

In these lines the poet dramatically introduces the theme of decay and uprooting in Eastern Europe. There are sounds of sorrow and of loud mourning rising above the scene in unbroken succession betokening the death and dissolution of a whole community which was once healthy and strong. Then comes the picture of the ghostly multitude of uprooted humanity—'the hooded hordes' wheeling about in an uneasy march over the arid plain which seems to be unending, with no goal within sight, but only the blue horizon visible in the distance all around it. It is a journey in the twilight dim atmosphere of a civilization on the brink of collapse, with the vision of the city on the mountain broken into atoms, which form and reform themselves before melting into the thin air. Even the ground under foot is breaking and many of the hopeless wanderers are falling and disappearing in the abyss which has yawned beneath. The dissolving city stands for the various capitals of Europe which have become ghostly appearances only with no sign of real life at their core.

The repetition of the epithet 'hooded', which is already used in respect of the resurrected Christ walking by the side of his intrigued disciples, in the context of this homeless human multitude is not without significance. In the first place it implies that the multitude is hardly human, being virtually a ghostly masquerade or a nightmare spectacle. Its deeper significance, however, will recall that these poor creatures, after all, belong to the Christian fold and are identified with the Saviour himself, who looked upon the oppressed humanity as identical with his own person, so much so that the sight of poor men and women, foodless and shelterless, made him exclaim that while birds and beasts have shelter the son of man has no where to rest his head on. It means, therefore, that the plight of the 'hooded hordes' is symbolical of the homeless, shelterless conditon of Christ himself, because, as Ruskin has finely said, where one hand meets another in love and fellowship there you have the true Church, the home of God. Banish love and sympathy for man, you are banishing God himself from your society.

'A woman drew her long black hair out tight etc.' introduces the image of Eastern Europe as an old mother gone mad with the deaths of her children and the break up of their homes, a modern Rachel lamenting the loss of her progeny. The picture is based upon the description in the German work we have quoted already and 'the old woman in delirium, singing hymns of death' appears here as an insane woman fiddling her subdued music on her own stretched hair—black but symptomatic of decay—as if it were a musical instrument. The mad song chimes in with the physical surroundings—blackened walls on which 'bats with baby faces are crawling downward down'. This is the picture of a civilization at its sun-set—'the violet light', with its once solid components fallen into sordid wrecks. The Church itself has felt the effect of the universal decay and its main function has become topsy-turvy. Its bells are still ringing as a token of the service which used to be performed there. But now the form merely is kept up, Christianity has declined into what Ruskin has called 'Churchianity'. People are still going to the Church and singing the conventional hymns, but they are the voices of godless men living in an 'empty cistern' and 'dry wells'. The lines obviously refer to a biblical text—*Jeremiah,* 2:13, 'My people have committed two evils; they have forsaken me, (saith the Lord), the fountain of living waters, and hewed them out cisterns, broken cisterns that can hold no water". It means that the modern humanity has rejected its God, the fountain-head of its strength and tranquillity and has decided to follow the mirage of luxury and sensual pleasures, which leave the heart 'high sorrowful and a parched tongue'.

'In this decayed hole among the mountains' etc. the scene now shifts to the stage of fulfilment in the mythical journey to Chapel Perilous. The Knight and his followers have weathered all difficulties and trials and have, at long last, reached their goal only to find the home of God fallen into decay with the wind sweeping through its rotten windows, while the graves around it are in the last stage of decay, with the bones of the dead peeping through the gaping holes and cracks. But now the questers have been able to make their truce with the dead, the 'sneering voices' have been silenced and the dead bones have lost their power to disturb them. The night of trials is over, the moon is shining and the grass is singing now in a different tune. Above all, the clarion note of the cock, 'Co Co rico' is heard of a sudden in the silent atmosphere, chasing the evil spirits and heralding the morn and the advent of rain-showers preceded by flashes of lightning and a welcome gust of damp wind. So the re-birth of the dead land and rejuvenation of the maimed King have become almost certain and there is a strong possibility of the rehabilitation of the old chapel and restoration of the suspended religious life. All these go together and only a living community can build a real Church.

Critics have drawn our attention to the biblical association of the crowing of the cock with the betrayal of Christ by Peter, but the associatson does not appear to be quite pertinent to this context, which is primarily concerned with a point in the progress of the spirit where reconciliation with God is expected rather than his betrayal.

But what about the aimless journey of the 'hooded hordes' in the modern wasteland ; The poet's answer to this question is implied in the passage which follows. Eliot commends the wisdom of the past as a remedy for the modern impasse because a people cannot live without their history, and the meaning of history is one of the major occupations of his philosophical poetry. 'History is servitude, history is freedom', here we have the whole problem in a nut-shell. The 'servitude' of history is the theme of *Gerontion*, because history there seems to have no centre and no pattern and appears to be a deceiving elf. This servitude can be converted into freedom if we are able to discover some timeless moments in history which give meaning to human life and human endeavours and bring the past into a fruitful union with the present. These moments are the moments of suffering, when humanity comes face to face with some crisis of the spirit and is hard put to it to find out some way of tiding over it. The remedy discovered or devised in such moments has a permanent value and validity in asmuch as pain and suffering abide in human life in all ages.

The remedy suggested here is the gift of the hoary wisdom of India which was found fruitful in a period of great spiritual crisis. It so happened that the holy land of the Hindus was once overtaken by drought, the water of the Ganges had touched the lowest mark, the leaves of trees were hanging down. the branches of trees bent low, and the whole forest was assuming a stooping posture, as it were, to sustain the force of the thunder-shower which was eagerly awaited and was quite imminent in view of the dark clouds mustertng in force over the Himalayas. This is the picture of a spiritual crisis in Indian culture of which the Ganges is the very bloodstream and the sinking of its water is naturally symptomatic of the low vitality of the spirit in the Indian community. Eliot refers to a significant episode in *The Brihadāraṇyaka Upanishad* which describes how in a moment of doubt and confusion, men, gods and demons approached Prajapati, the giver of all wisdom, for guidance. In answer to their prayer the divine teacher uttered in thunder only one Sanskrit word thrice—Da, Da, Da, which each group interpreted in its own peculiar way as *Datta, Dayadhvam* and *Damayat*, give, sympathise and control. As man himself is the single centre of all the three properties—human, angelic and demonic, the terms may be taken together to form the three-fold path of deliverance from the darkness and sterility of the spiritual life.

Now each of the three remedies is applied to the condition of the modern humanity with a view to revealing the utter lack of those virtues which are always vital for the human race. What is the meaning of 'give' in relation to humanity ? Giving does not mean charity or distribution of alms among the poor. The poet takes it in the sense of giving oneself away, a positive commitment in a moment of great emotional conviction—'blood shaking my heart'. In the life of man there arise moments when hesitation, prudence and dilatory discussions of pros and cons are quite out of place. Man has to surrender to the dictates of his throbbing and clamouring heart and take a plunge into the dark. This is the positive commitment to a way of life dictated by the wisdom of a full-blooded heart which no later prudence can nullify. This 'giving' to the insistent demand of the great occasions has oonstituted the real life of humanity; it has been behind all revolutions, all adventures of body and mind; it has sent martyrs singing to the flames and patriots to the gallows and has given even to Satan 'courage never to submit or yield' even though the field has been lost. Eliot has rightly remarked that 'it is better to do evil than nothing, at least we exist'. By this attitude we have existed and it is this attitude which is becoming rarer in our age of emotional emaciation. In the well-known article, *The Archetypal Imagery of T. S. Eliot* (P.M.L.A., Vol. 60, 1945, pp. 567-585), Mr. G. W. Foster has quoted a significant observation of Dr. Harding:

"The voice of the thunder in *Wasteland* speaks not only of the emotional problems of modern man as an individual but also of world problems in a century where the almost exclusive concern with masculine and mechanical concepts of life has well-nigh choked the springs of living water which are gifts of the feminine principle of Eros." (Page 575).

In the concluding part of *The Prelude* William Wordsworth affirms that Love and Imagination are inseparable and cannot be divided. Love is an inner-possession, the personal property of man which nothing external to him can shape or provide Eliot also implies that this emotional commitment—'the awful daring of a moment's surrender'—is an inner achievement, pure and simple, and will not be counted among his external actions and possessions. It will not appear in the account of his life in the newspaper, after his death, nor will it find mention in the account of his wealth and assets, recorded in his last will and testament left behind him, the seal of which will be broken by his 'lean solicitor' in his death chamber empty of him; it will perhaps find no place in the inscription on his tombstone, the record and epitome of his life and achievement, which in course of time will be covered by the 'beneficent spiders'. The last phrase glances at a remark in Webster's *White Devil*, 'ere the spider makes a thin curtain for your epitaphs'.

Dayadhvam—sympathise, is an emotional going out of one's own ego into the mind of somebody else—an emotional bond of union between two persons or between the individual and the group. But the humanity of to-day has become ego-centric and we 'modern millions live alone'. The remark of Count Ugolino (I have heard the key turn in the door) in Dante's *Inferno* is a fit summary of the present-day humanity. He tells Dante that he was thrust into the tower and the door was locked and communication with the external world completely cut off. So in our wasteland each man is confined to his own ego-cell and is impervious to the impressions outside. Our talk of the necessity of breaking this narrow cell and of the remedies conducive to the wider outlook, go to show that we are self-centred and ego-centric. Eliot refers to a remark of Bradley, author of *Appearance and Reality*, to support this point of view: "My external sensations are no less private to myself than are my thoughts and my feelings. In either case, my experience falls within my own circle, a circle closed on the outside; and, with all its elements alike, every sphere is opaque to the others which surround it. In brief, regarded as an existence which appears in a soul, the whole world for each is peculiar to that soul'. 'Only at a nightfall ...... a broken Coriolanus.' This self-imprisoned humanity gets out of the walls of its ego only in the silence of the night, under the drowsy numbness which overpowers the conscious ego and makes the passage smooth for the upward swing of the unconscious feelings, the conventional Christian feelings, 'ethereal rumours', forgotten by our waking consciousness, and for a moment our callous heart is ready to admit the sentiments of love and sympathy, so that the condition of 'broken Coriolanus' is revived. 'Broken Coriolanus' has a double association. In Shakespeare's Roman play named afterr him he is presented as a proud, self-centred and arrogant aristocrat who admits pity and becomes heart-broken, however briefly, under the persuasion of his commanding mother. The second association is more personal and relates to the two poems composed by Eliot round this Roman leader and statesman. In both of them he is apparently a man of action standing in the centre of pomp and political activities, but his heart is divided between two loyalties, loyalty to his external duty and loyalty also to a deeper order or sphere of reality which he can glimpse even in moments of hectic activity :

> "Hidden in the stillness of noon, in the silent croaking night.
>
> Come with the sweep of the little bat's wing, with the small flare of firefly or lightning bug.

The small creatures chirp thinly through the dust,
through the night.

Damayat,—control, emphasizes the necessity of regulating the heart 'shaking with blood' in such a way that discipline curtails no whit of freedom—'as they move easiest who have learnt to dance'. The heart under such a discipline is imaged as the gay boat gliding freely under the expert hands of sailors in Wagner's *Tristan and Isolde*. This is the fruit of inner discipline adopted spontaneously by heart to get above the reach of the sensuous urges which draw a person into the ocean. The Phoenician sailor was drowned for lack of such a discipline. Jung has reminded us that ocean is the primordial symbol of the subconscious and also of the life of the senses. It is a strong ocean, terrible and destructive for those who are without discipline, but for a disciplined heart the sea is calm and placid and the voyage a gay adventure without risk and fear.

The closing lines, which have been declared by some critics as a farrago of meaningless fragments, contain really the core of the poem, the point of convergence of the scattered meditations of the protagonist. They strike a personal note, the Protagonist becoming the mouth-piece of the poet himself, who is fishing or searching for spiritual fertility, turning his back upon the 'arid plain' or the spiritually barren society. As the social structure is breaking down (London bridge is falling down), the sensitive individual will have to take the initiative for the reconstruction of his own spiritual life (set my lands in order). So he selects three fragments from the broken culture of the West for personal reconstruction, which correspond to the three key-words of Indian Upanishad, discussed already, as the triple way of social deliverance, The three fragments, which the artist has 'shored against his ruin', contain the germs of the poet's own philosophy which he later elaborates in the *Four Quartets:* The first refers to the words of Araunt Daniel to Dante in *Purgatorio.* He is suffering in purgatory but is glad to think that the flames will purify his soul. So he leaves with the prayer: 'please remember my pain'. So, for the poet the first step is the acceptance of suffering as a way of purifying the soul—a cardinal creed with Eliot. This leads to the Latin fragment taken from the beautiful poem, *Pervigilium Veneris*, the Eve of Venus, which celebrates the return of spring, a season of new life and freedom when the birds are pouring their songs with 'full-throated ease'. The poet alone is tongue-tied, but yearns for a like release; the nightingale sings, her cruel memories forgotten and the poet says', 'when will spring awaken in me? When shall I be as the swallow, that I may cease to be voiceless. The nightingale and swallow, for Eliot, are symbols of beauty, purity and freedom, born of suffering willingly undergone. The tongueless Philomel became the nightingale of 'inviolable song' and in the swallow the cruel and bereaved mother emerged as the light-hearted lover of spring and summer in Swinburne and, more importantly still, the bird of consolation' in the Christian legend. So the second fragment stresses the hope of the sufferer that it will lead him to beauty and freedom. This suffering-purification-release-and joy is the way up of the mystic John of the Cross. The opposite way, equally important in the spiritual discipline, is the way down, the way of utter destitution. The third fragment is derived from a sonnet by Gerard de Nerval, the poet bereft of every thing, like the Prince of Acquitaine at the ruined tower, has no stay and is yet hopeful about his life. This stage is the negative aspect of the same discipline, utter destitution of the soul of all attachment for worldly things which is a pre-requisite for the soul's progress towards a new life. We may recall here a remark of Jung which illuminates this third state of the spirit: "All creativeness in the realm of spirit......arises from a state of mental suffering, and it is spiritual stagnation, psychic sterility which causes this state".

Thus, like Hieronymo, the poet is fitting out a play of well-arranged parts, and he is sure to be taken for a mad man by the people around him who have lost faith in spiritual values. But just as Hieronymo found strength in his madness which made him oblivious of his grief, so this spiritual madness constitutes the one resource of the poet to reconstruct his own inner life which combined with '*Datta, Dayadhvam, Damayat*', the formula for social reconstruction, will make the benediction of heaven descend on the tormented humanity like the refreshing drops of gentle rain, 'Shantih, Shantih, Shantih', and lead his own soul to a state of that repose which 'passeth comprehension'.

GENERAL REMARKS

TECHNIQUE AND STYLE

In this concluding part we shall examine at length certain salient aspects of the poem, which we have already briefly touched upon in the introductory part. The technique of *The Waste Land* reflects its author's lively awareness of some of the major movements in the intellectual, philosophical and scientific spheres of the modern world, which were already shaping the art and literature of the age in England as well as on the continent. Notable among such movements were the developments in Anthropology and Psychology, in Physics and Philosophy, where Einstein had joined hands with Bergson to develop a new concept of time which obliterated the barrier between past and present and future and subsumed the periods anterior and posterior into the eternal present. The idea found support in the technique of the modern popular amusement, the cinema, with its aptness to present all periods, places and events simultaneously.

Anthropology and Psychology were at one in their emphasis upon the significance of myth as the earliest and the most spontaneous and collective effort of human communities to order the life of the individual and of the entire community through a fruitful relationship between individual and society and between man and nature around him on the one hand and on the other between man and supernatural forces which were by no means less real or less close to the human life. This interpretation of myth easily paved the way for the cultivation of the mythical method which Eliot has explained in his essay on Joyce's *Ulysses*, cited already in the introductory part of this section, as a way of imposing order on the vast panorama of anarchy and chaos which is contemporary history. It is the way of juxtaposing and telescoping the past and the present and under-scoring the timeless quality of the myth. This simultaneous presentation of the ages gone by and the age in which we are living accounts for two major peculiarities of the poems in which the myths are used. In the first place, the mythical method may produce a circular structure, which is a certainty if the myth happens to be a story of death and re-birth; and secondly, the mythical method is characterized by the devices of parallelism and contrast which stress at once the points in common between the past and the present and the ways in which they are demonstrably unlike each other.

These features are not peculiar only to *The Waste Land* but may be discovered in all poems old and new where a myth of death and re-birth forms the framework or the living core. The point has received support, for example, from the recent studies of Milton's *Paradise Lost* as 'myth'. It has been pointed out that Milton was the great inheritor of the Renaissance tradition, with its interpretation of old myths quite similar to our own. In this tradition a distinction was made between 'perfect history' which is the central story of man's fall and redemption in Christianity, and the 'crooked history' which comprises all the events and developments in the life of the race of Adam since his fall and exile from Eden. As Milton takes this archetypal 'myth' as the theme of his poetry he is perfectly justified in pressing the later myths, historical events, persons, and things, by way of similes and comparisons, into his service to define and distinguish the characters and the events in his great epic. Moreover, Milton uses parallelism and contrast within the poem itself. Satan and the fallen angels are cast out of the kingdom of heaven and decide to adopt 'evil' for their 'good' to despite God. Yet they try to build a kingdom in Hell in conscious imitation of God's heaven. Satan sits exalted on his throne like God, surrounded by his followers who offer him service, allegiance and unquestioned loyalty. The Pandemonium is built by Mammon in the likeness of the golden seat of the angels with the only difference, as Dr. Rajan has shrewdly pointed out, that gold which forms the floor of heaven is found glittering on the ceiling and roof of the infernal fabric. Similarly Satan—Sin—Death relationship is the hellish counterpart of the holy Trinity in heaven. A similar parallelism, with implied contrast, can be seen between the fall of Lucifer and the fall of Adam. Adam and Eve in Eden stand as the counterparts of Lucifer and Sin in heaven. Sin is born out of the head of Satan and

Eve is formed out of the bleeding rib of Adam. The part played by the feminine partners are strikingly similar because love turned into lust is a primary factor in both the stories. 'The act of darkness done with sin begins in a dark midnight in Heaven, moves towards a night temptation in Eden and ends in eternal darkness visible in Hell', as Mr. Jackson Cope. author of '*The Metaphoric Structure of Paradise Lost*', has put it. Milton is at pains to identify the hell of Satan with the fall of Adam. The repentant Adam pours his woe into the ears of his vain partner:...into what Abyss of fears

> And horros hast thou driv'n me, out of which
> I find no way, from deep to deeper plunged.

Here the key-words, 'Abyss', 'horrors', 'deep' and 'plunged' are used as the unmistakable links between this hell and the vast deep into which Satan and his host are plunged by God.

A word may also be said about the structure of the great epic. We expect here the conventional narrative movement peculiar to the epic, yet the central myth of sin and redemption, death and re-birth, effectively moulds it into a more or less circular form. The forecast is given in the invocation itself which mentions not only the sin and its fruit, the death, but also the promise of redemption leading to the regaining of that 'blissful seat' from which Adam and Eve were expelled—thus, the end of man is actually his beginning, The point is further clarified by God who can easily view the whole course of human destiny at a single glance. It is true that in the body of of the epic Satan starts on a journey, yet his voyage is vertical rather than horizontal. He rises up from Hell and Chaos upto Heaven and Eden but eventually falls back into the depth from which he had started.

It is now time to pass to *The Wastc Land* and examine its mythical technique which is much more complex and ingenious than in Milton's epic. Eliot constructs a mythical framework by cunningly weaving together the wastelands in the three important traditions of European Culture. The Mediaeval wasteland of the Fisher King is linked with the classical wasteland of Oedipus King through Tiresias and both again with the 'evil land' in the Bible, a country without water and without green trees. This complex framework is brought into juxtaposition with the contemporary wasteland which offers a striking similarity to them in all the essentials. In all of them the emphasis falls on sin and its consequence, death, from which one way of redemption is the purgatory of suffering accepted willingly and with joy for the purification of the soul. One aspect of this sin is the disregard of the sanctity of sex which leads to the orgies and perversions of lust, turning the relation of man and woman into the biological and thoughtless coupling of animals under the pressure of natural instincts. Further parallelism between the present and the past is found, firstly, in the identification of the 'London crowd' with the crowd in Dante's Hell and Limbo, where men who had denied their God, and men who had led a negative existence merely, are doomed to dwell and the crowd in the modern 'unreal city' of dim atmosphere is their exact counterpart; secondly, men and women in the modern wasteland, who are living simply on animal planes, pursuing the bubbles of earthly glory and pleasures of the senses, become simply a type of worldly creatures in all ages when life loses its height and depth and the senses swallow the spirit. When the Buddha and Augustine, representatives of the wisdom of East and West, visualized humanity as burning in the flames of fire, they had such men and women in mind. In this way the poet moves on linking the present with the past and extending the meaning of the modern wasteland.

At the same time the contrast between the past and the present is quite glaring and has been constantly emphasized in the poem. Man has never been a perfect creature and every age of human history has been guilty of those follies and crimes which are disfiguring the life of the race in the present age. Yet in the days gone by there was a fairly wide-spread faith in a set of moral and religious values which constituted the permanent standard for measuring the dignity and degradation of society. This faith gave a depth and sanctity to every object of nature and every activity of man, lending to human existence itself a double layer of meaning, literal as well as spiritual. Thus, spring and winter, fire and water, sowing and reaping, washing, bathing and drowning, the union of men and women, the drought and rainfall etc. were given a spiritual depth below their apparent surface. This naturally brought into being a number of rituals and ceremonies connected with the events of social and individual life where this belief was actually enacted.

But to-day these values have become 'a heap of broken images' or 'withered stumps of time', the universal feeling of sanctity has disappeared and life has been reduced to the literal surface. Water is now merely destructive and so is fire, winter and spring have become mere seasons to be welcomed or avoided by man to suit his own convenience. At places the poet produces the shock of ironic contrast by picturing the literal aspect of certain activities in the contemporary world, while keeping their deeper significance clearly in the background. Thus, Mrs. Porter and her daughter wash their feet in soda-water, a travesty of the ritual washing of feet; the bones of the Phoenician sailor are caught by the current of water and carried into the whirlpool, in obvious contrast to the ritualistic drowning of the fertility gods which led to a new and fruitful life. The ironic contrast becomes shockingly bathetic in:

> When a lovely woman stoops to folly
>
> ....
>
> She smooths her hair with automatic hand
> And puts a record on the gramophone.

It is not necessary to catalogue all the instances of this contrast and we shall end with a reference to the universal idea of human life as a journey, not only physical but more significantly spiritual. In the fifth movement two fruitful journeys are sharply contrasted with the fruitless march of uprooted humanity in the modern wasteland. In the first two the desert of doubt and death was by no means absent but the goal was fixed for man and he had faith in the power of suffering to purify his soul and make the desert bloom again with life. But the confused multitude of to-day has lost its goal of life and 'ringed by flat horizon only' the wretches composing it can only stumble and fall into the 'cracked earth'.

This brings us to the apparently circular structure of the poem determined partly by its theme of death and re-birth. It has been pointed out that the poem opens with the picture of the dry mountainous landscape 'where the sun beats and dead tree gives no shelter, the cricket no relief and dry stones no sound of water'; and its end brings us back to the arid plain, where London bridge is falling down and the 'unreal city' is breaking and dissolving, while 'bats with baby faces' are crawling down and down the blackened walls of the broken civilization. From this it has been concluded that the poem makes no progress towards a definite goal, but comes round to the point from which it had started.

> "The progress in *The Waste Land*, for there is progress, is not the progress of narrative movement along a line, the progress of an Odyssus towards his home or of Bunyan's pilgrim from the City of Destruction to the Celestial City; it is like the progress of Langland in *Piers Plowman*, the greatest visionary poem in England......In both poems we are not, however, moving in a circle but on a spiral up and down, 'the way up is the way down.'

Throughout we come back continually to the same point at different levels."

(Helen Gardner: *The Art of T. S. Eliot*, pp. 96-97).

We have also been told that the poem adopts a musical structure, that it is a symphony of five movements in which certain themes and counter-themes are worked out in a 'contrapuntal movement' each movement taking us deeper into the heart of the subject. To this view I. A. Richards has set a seal of approval with his remark that *The Waste Land* is 'a music of ideas'.

Yet when all this has been accepted by a discerning reader he will still remain in the 'palpable obscure' of half-understanding if he fails to perceive the gradual shifting of the point through the five movements in a progressive way within the circular structure, which means that the circular structure or spiral movement of the poem does carry us insensibly, it may be, from one point to another in a straight line, tracing the progress of the spirit from total death to the grey light of a new-birth, which may be still far off. In this way the basic circular pattern of the death-rebirth myth is not fully realized, though the remaining part of the curve is not entirely hard to perceive. We notice three crucial points in the inner movement of the basic idea in the poem, namely, progress from spiritual barrenness towards spiritual reconstruction. In the beginning we stand in the heart of the kingdom of death where rocks are breaking to fragments and there is no sound of water and hardly any possibility of the birth and growth of new life. In the second stage which comes at the beginning of the fifth movement the rocks are still there but the longing for water has become an agony of the spirit which has come to realize its paramount necessity or significance:

If there were water
    And no rock
If there were rock
    And also water
And water
    A spring
A pool among the rock
If there were the sound of water only.

But by the time we reach thc closing part—I sat fishing—the poem has moved a step further. The arid plain has gone behind and water has come in front of the protagonist who is intent on fishing. The sound of things breaking, of London bridge falling down, is haunting his ear, but he is determined to set at least his own land in order by shoring three fragments against his ruin which will become the corner-stone of his personal regeneration, while society must adopt the threefold path of spiritual deliverance—*Datta, Dayadhvam, Damayat*, if it wants peace to descend upon its tormented spirit like drops of a gentle, life-giving rain.

In *American Poetry Since 1900*, Mr. Louis Untermeyer has been pleased to remark about the nature of *The Waste Land* as follows:

> "It is doubtful whether *The Waste Land* is any thing but a set of separate poems, a piece of literary carpentary, scholarly joiner's work, the flotsam and

jetsam of dessicated culture.........a pompous parade of erudition."

The criticism is as positive as it is unjust and in its sweeping dogmatism can not fail to remind one of Dr. Johnson's criticism of the Metaphysical poets. It betrays a total disregard, unconscious or deliberate, of the poet's intention which is implied in his preference for the mythical method, defined as a way of controlling or imposing order upon the vast panorama of chaos or moral anarchy which is contemporary history. His aim throughout has been to relate the modern disorganized society to the larger European tradition, which will always remain its root. There is nothing reactionary in this emphasis when we remember that in the human psyche itself there is a most primitive part which cannot be forgotten and in all crises of life the individual or social psyche has to be renewed through a fruitful contact with this dark ocean within, which Jung has described as the creative mother of the conscious part.

Eliot has, likewise, argued that the past is a vital part of the present, even though it is supposed to be dead; that human history has a pattern of 'timeless' moments whose truth and validity are eternal. One of such moments is concerned with the recurrence of the periods of low spiritual vitality in human society and in individual life when earnest effort has to be made by sensitive souls to remedy their own ills and prepare the ground for social salvation as well.

Eliot thus looks upon the human predicament in the contemporary world as a familiar phase of human history, which can be remedied by the application of the wisdom which has already been tried and tested in the past. If you call it old-fashioned the poet would retort that there is nothing in the uptodate view of modern life which promises to save the soul of man or which redounds to the dignity of his nature. What his critics have described as 'dessicated' fragments are the sound bricks of the shattered culture of East and West which can be joined together to build the fabric of the spiritual values without which all material and scientific advance will mean a progressive going back from God towards the Dust.

'Surely the great poet is', says Eliot in *Use of Poetary and Use of Criticism*, 'among other things, one who not merely restores a tradition which has been in abeyance, but one who in his poetry re-twines as many straying strands of tradition as possible'. This is an accurate description of the poet's intention in joining the fragments of cultures in the poem. The joining is not mechanical but organic because it makes a whole of meaning and gives inner coherence to the apparently incoherent poem. Thus, in the mythical framework the wastelands of different ages—mediaeval, classical, biblical and even Indian—are united together to stress the basic fact that the modern phenomenon is only a recurring problem of human history, Similarly, the Buddha's view of physical existence is collocated with the utterances of St. Augustine in order simply to show the universality of the wisdom which the poet opposes to the materialism of his age. To give, to sympathise, to control are the vital principles of life which their association with the hoary past of a foreign race does not render stale or unacceptable. If the poet shores three fragments from the dead culture of Europe to save himself he simply wishes us to realize that they are the symbols of abiding truth which age cannot wither and which is lost frequently but has to be recovered again and again. Eliot's fragments, therefore, cohere to make a fairly clear and sound philosophy of life which can be disregarded or disparaged only by those who are still clinging to the faith that science is not only our good fairy but also our godmother even in the face of the searing experience of the victims of this goddess in Hiroshima and Nagasaki.

This leads us to the ticklish problem raised by the critics of Eliot, whether the poem ends on a note of hope or despair. The answer to this question will depend upon the point on which we focus our attention. If, for example, we consider the problem from the poet's personal point of view we shall have little difficulty in concluding that the poet is quite hopeful. He has explored the depth of the spiritual abyss only as the most important first step in his pilgrimage towards life and light. The acute awareness of the dark abyss leads him to think of the ways and means of setting at least his own land in order, and the three fragments shored by him form the foundation of a creative attitude in which suffering born of sin has to be gladly accepted as the fire of purgatory which purifies the soul and makes it fit for the love of God. Eliot's later poetry shows this spiritual progress.

But the case seems to be quite different with the people of the wasteland who are not only unaware of their condition but quite glad and content with their depleted life, 'feeding a little life with dried tubers'. For such persons, who are sitting in 'the stye of contentment, that is Death', even the wisdom of the past concentrated in the Upanishadic formula—*Datta, Dayadhvam, Damayat'* is meaningless. There is only one saving grace, however, that the human mind has always been noted for its resilience; it has sinned and gone into the abyss but only to strive to get out of it. If the present is in an essential sense an extension of the past of humanity with notable additions, of course, one cannot lose all hope even for modern humanity.

In reply to the critical verdict that the poem deals with the disillusionment of a generation, Eliot reportedly remarked that 'it deals with their illusion of being disillusioned'. What the poet precisely meant by this cryptic remark is not easy to determine but this much can be stated, without fear of contradiction, that the poem is well calculated to appeal to the conscience of the sensitive men and women in our age of anxiety, to induce them to search their hearts and to realize the spiritual bankruptcy of a civilization which is committed wholly and unreservedly to the material values and creature-comforts without any serious concern for the higher ideals and profounder convictions.

This brings us to an important aspect of the technique and style, namely, the devices employed by the poet to effect the merger of the present and the past and link the contemporary problem with other epochs of cultural and literary history of Europe in particular and of humanity in general. In this respect the role of Tiresias, as the symbol of human consciousness, is the first consideration of great significance which we have briefly explained in the introductory part. To this we may add an illuminating remark of Lawrence Durrell which emphasizes the cinematographic technique of the poem: "Tiresias is the camera-man, then. But he is not fixed chronologically—he can move about in history and in time, he can become a modern city-man, a mediaeval, or an ancient Greek at will. *The Waste Land* is his spiritual autobiography, his search through the junk-heap of modern culture for an integrating principle.........And the camera moves backwards and forwards with a relentless shuttling movement over legend, belief and symbol. No sooner does it pick a figure than it dissolves into its attributes......Eliot's characters, like many Greek gods, enjoy multiple attributes, often opposing ones".

(*Key to Modern Poetry*, p. 133)

Little wonder, therefore, that Tiresias should speak many languages and thus fully justify the poet's use of a device which has been aptly described as Eliot's *poettc short-hand*, that is, the device of linking London with places and scenes in history, myth and literature by mere introduction of phrases or fragments of quotations from poets and authors of other countries and ages. Thus a single phrase of Baudelaire, 'unreal city', identifies London with Paris, and a single line of his makes Stetson a representative of modern humanity of low aims and material outlook. In the same way with the help of a couple of quotations from Dante's *Inferno* the poet is able to convert the London crowd of clerks and businessmen into the multitude of doomed men loitering near the Hell as they had lived 'without praise or blame' and were not positive enough to be even of the Devil's party to earn a place in his infernal kingdom. We have already pointed out how a number of biblical echoes in the central passage of the opening section, 'Son of man, you cannot say or guess', transform the modern wasteland into the evil land of the Scripture where sinful humanity is panic-stricken with the fear of death. We may also direct the attention of the reader to the opening lines in the second movement of the poem—'A Game of Chess'—where the modern lady of fashion and frayed nerves is linked by this device to Shakespeare's Cleopatra, Virgil's Dido, to Lamia, Imogen, Eve, Philomela and the host of fatal women patronised by the Romantic and decadent art and literature, while the sex-duel of to-day becomes the sordid game of chess in Middleton's *Women Beware Women.*

The device is also effective for producing a sudden sense of ironic contrast between the past values and the present lack of them. Thus, the mechanical intercourse of the typist and her young man carbuncular receives a powerful illumination through its sudden juxtaposition with the moral ideal embodied in Goldsmith's moving song, 'When a lovely woman stoops to folly'. The behaviour of the typist becomes a heartless parody of the serious view of chastity and its loss which inspires the original song. Similarly, 'Sounds of horns' etc. in the third movement brings the noble Greek world sharply in contrast with our vulgar civilization where Actaeon has degenerated into Mr. Sweeney and goddess Diana into Mrs. Porter whose washing of her feet in soda-water is a cheap and unconscious travesty of bathing and washing which anciently were rich in sacred implications. This holds good also in respect of spring, winter, burial and planting of the corpse and drowning in water where the imagination switches swiftly from the single literal plane of to-day to the richer dual vision of ancient humanity which transfigured these ordinary objects and operations with spiritual enrichment.

It is, I think, neither arbitrary nor unreasonable to consider the employment of *symbols and imagery* also under the technique of the poetic shorthand. It is not necessary in this brief discussion to enter into the subtle shades of distinction which scholars have been at pains to discover between 'symbol' and 'imagery'. We shall only content ourselves with the remark that in both the cases certain objects and even facts of life become associated with certain feelings and ideas and can be used in place of them, with the only difference that imagery is extended, while 'symbol' is concentrated; while the one may be clearly indicative of a single idea, the other has a greater complexity of association. A symbol is like a pebble cast into a pool of water causing a succession of wavelets, one following the other, in a series of concentric circles. Eliot has pointed out that in course of our life certain objects and scenes may become associated with our feelings and experiences and thus acquire a symbolic value for us. The symbolic style thus is obviously conducive to economy, indirectness, concentrated effect and a great emotional and spiritual intensity which no amount of direct statement can ever hope to produce. What is true of the experience of the individual is also true—true perhaps in a greater measure—of the experiences of the race. Man in community has lived for a long time in close association with nature and the objects of the external world till they were enriched with profound association with his deepest feelings. So when the occasion came for man to express his deep religious feelings and spiritual or mystic experiences he had to fall back upon his sensuous experiences and the phenomenal world familiar to him and work out a complicated device of 'correspondences', making the familiar objects and experiences the intelligible media for thoughts and experiences too profound to be articulated in ordinary language. In this way, sun, moon, mountain, river, ocean, drought and rainfall, journey, voyage, fire and air, summer and winter, sowing and growing, birds, beasts and flowers become symbols of great value in myth, reli gion, magic, alchemy and mystery-cults as well as occult practices. The discoveries of Freud and Jung have lent great support to the significance of such symbols and images in the life of the race and of the individual.

Jung, especially, has bridged the gulf between science on the one hand and art, religion and literature on the other, by pointing out that a large tract of the unconscious layer may be described as the 'Collective Unconscious', because it is the reservoir of primordial images representing the survival of race-memories in the mind of the individual. These archetypal images are activised in the mental life of the sophisticated individuals if the psyche reaches a stage of crisis or turning-point, so that a modern man may encounter images of myth and primitive religions in his dreams, when the sub-conscious is more free and more active.

Thus, the mythical motives have been studied psychologically and the development of Eliot's own poetry in terms of death and rebirth has been explained on the principle of Jungian archetypes by Elizabeth Drew, Maud Bodkin and a number of discerning psychologists.

The poet, thus, may draw upon the stocks of conventional images and symbols, or not satisfied with them, he may contrive a set of personal symbols of which he alone has the key. If this happens on a large scale the readers are completely at his mercy for making out his meaning. The philosophical Poetry of W. B. Yeats is a familiar example of this practice, but the most characteristic and disconcerting illustrations are afforded by the French symbolist poets, headed by Mallarme'.

Eliot was influenced by the symbolist technique but could not concur with its masters in creating an opaque aura of obscure and personal images and symbols between the readers and the poems. Most of his images are conventional, drawn from myth, religion and nature, with only a very small percentage of images which appear to have been either contrived by himself or made complex through the device of adding and compounding or profoundly modifying the familiar images. In *The Waste Land* examples of the latter are not numerous, but one may cite 'the red rock', 'the Dog' and 'broken Coriolanus' as fair samples of the class. In this poem the images and symbols fall broadly into two categories—firstly, images drawn from myth and religion, and secondly, images taken from the common aspects of urban life, quite trite in appearance but raised to great intensity by the emotional pressure behind them, a device which he found and admiringly studied in Baudelaire and Laforgue. We may refer to the image of 'a taxi throbbing and waiting' used with great effect to epitomise the life of the typist; and 'the silk hat on the head of Bradford millionaire' to typify the awkward posture of 'assurance' of the otherwise low mind of the young man carbuncular.

The list may also include the image used by one of the Thames-daughters to convey the sense of utter emptiness in her life—the past as well as the present—'I can connect nothing with nothing, the broken finger nails of a dirty hand.'

But the majority of the most significant symbols is drawn from myth and religion and is centred round the basic theme of death and re-birth. Thus spring stands for re-birth and winter for death; drought is symbolic of spiritual dryness and rain of spiritual fertility; the hard rock breaking under the sun may typify spiritual disintegration, while water and fish may well stand for the fertility, growth and rejuvenation of the spirit. Yet, here we shall do well to bear in mind the obvious fact that certain objects may symbolize two opposite ideas based upon their different functions; thus, water is an ambivalent symbol because it is, in the first place, a symbol of creation, of life and growth, of purification and transformation into something rich and strange. On the other hand, in the shape of a river or sea, it is also destructive of life and property; it may suck up a man into the vortex and pound even huge ships into fragments. This is why the ocean is a symbol of the world with its temptations and also of the sub-conscious and the life of the senses in which a person may get lost. Similarly, fire is apparently a destructive agent and has been quite properly employed by the Buddha, Augustine and all teachers and preachers as a symbol of lust and desire, which consume a person in a state of 'living death'. But fire is also the sacred altar-flame symbol of inspiration, illumination and spiritual exaltation and ecstasy. Eliot constantly plays with this ambivalence behind spring, winter, fire, water, drowning and washing etc. to indicate the fundamental difference between the life on the literal plane purely in the wasteland and life lived on the double plane of sense and spirit in the mythical and religious past.

This ambivalence is also latent in such primary symbols as burial of the dead, planting of the corpse, life as journey and voyage.

We are now in a position to study the effectiveness of Eliot's complex symbolic technique which serves to vivify the various aspects of life in modern wasteland, which occupies the centre of the poem: Eliot uses appropriate images to emphasize the state of spiritual death and deterioration in the post-war European society. Thus, its spiritual sterility is underscored by the picture of a stony and barren soil, where the sun beats and the dead tree gives ne shelter and there is no sound of water'. In such a soil, what roots can clutch, what branches grow ?' and who can be sure of the fact that the planted corpse will kindle into a new life in the face of the cold and frost and the destructive nails of the dog ? The fog in London reduces it to an 'unreal city' creating the dim atmosphere of Dante's Limbo, in which the crowd pouring over the London Bridge becomes a fit counterpart of the wretched spirits in *Inferno* who had been tied to a meaningless negative existence, 'without fame or infamy'. The heat of the scorching sun becomes hellish fire in the third movement where sense-ridden humanity gets its precise definition from the words of the Buddha and St. Augustine, 'burning, burning, burning', 'To Carthage then I came, O Lord! thou pluckest me' etc. Then, there is the idea of stalemate, of life come to a deadend, physically, mentally and sexually, of which 'The Game of Chess' in the second movement, is the most complex and emphatic symbol. With this is combined the idea of life as a prison, a meaningless, dull and languid movement in a narrow circle, pinpointed by a set of images—'we are living in a rat's alley where dead men lost thesr bones' or we hear the key turn, each in his prison, thinking of the key, each confirms the prison'. This idea is re-inforeed by the images indica tive of squalor and vulgarity, internal as well as external. Thus, the river sweats oil and tar and carries along its current the dirty freight of empty bottles, cigarette ends and silk handkerchiefs etc., testimonies of summer parties and sexual encounters between city-nymphs and their chance paramours, the sons and heirs of London merchants and Directors. The protagonist sits fishing in the dull canal behind the gas-house, while a rat crawls on its slimy belly through the rich vegetation, where white bodies dead and naked have been deposited by the stream of the river. Naturally, therefore, fear so peculiar to sinful humanity—'a handful of dust', under the judgement of God—'the red rock'—is a prevailing sentiment in this world. Fear of life and of death, fear in the 'languid ecstasy' of love satisfied and of the torment of love unsatisfied, which is contrasted with and re-inforced by the spiritual fear attending the soul in suffering in the final movement:

> **Red sullen faces sneer and snarl**
> **From the mud-cracked houses.**

Above all, there is the imagery of disintegration, physical and spiritual, which runs through several parts and practically envelops the whole: Thus, the rocks are breaking, the London bridge is falling down, the 'hooded hordes' are swarming over the plain with the earth cracking under their feet and the noise of the city dissolving in the air; a strong sense of the 'violet light of civilization' with its ruined black and broken walls and 'bats with baby faces crawling downward, down them and 'upturned towers with reminiscent bells and human voices singing in empty cisterns and exhausted wells.' It is a country of spiritual decay also where old values have become 'a heap of broken images' or 'withered stumps of time', where a lovely woman gets up after her sexual fall only to smooth her hair with 'automatic hand' and set a record on her gramophone and the sound of horns carries Mr. Sweeney, our modern Actaeon, to Mrs. Porter, our degraded Diana, who joins labour with her daughter not in a sacred bath or ritual purification but in washing the feet in soda-water.

The release from this state is also glimpsed in appropriate images: Thus, the sense of release and freedom is conveyed by the image of 'heart shaking with blood in the awful draing of a moment's surrender' and by that of a boat gliding smoothly under the expert hand; the end of trial and advent of hope are indicated by the crowing of the cock followed by a gust of damp wind bringing rain.

How far these images are the fit conventional and almost universal symbols of the basic concept of the spiritual death and re-birth can be clearly seen from a brief examination of the motives and their appropriate images employed by Coleridge in the *Rime of Ancient Mariner*, which deals with identical theme, but is quite patently at the opposite pole from *The Waste Land* in all other respects, style, technique, structure and diction. It is the soul of simplicity and naivety, while *The Waste Land* is the last word in complexity, intricacy and sophisticated atmosphere, combined with a pervasive erudite flavour. The very elements in which the poems move are different, the one is rooted in the stony landscape and the other is concerned with the voyage on the sea. The apparent contrast, however, serves to bring the basic likeness of the two poems into bolder relief. The Mariner, so strange and unhuman, is not unlike Tiresias, and his personal experiences have universal bearing, so that he becomes a type of sinning and suffering humanity, in a sense, Every Man. In both the poems the central theme has a strong mediaeval colouring, not only in the conception of Sin-death-penance-re-birth pattern, but also in the emphasis upon the interpenetration of human life and the universe of nature, where the degradation of man entails the disintegration in nature.

The pattern of death and re-birth followed in the two poems is the conventional Christian scheme, which is quite familiar also to the students of mythology and anthropology and can very well be presented, and it has been presented, in terms of analytical psychology also, as interpreted especially by Jung and his followers. Before entering into the details of symbols and motives common to the poems we shall do well to keep in mind an important reservation in regard to the relationship between the physical and symbolical significances of the objects employed as key-terms to workout the common theme. In the *Rime* the objects of nature, sun, moon, water, rain etc. strike us more immediately as the familiar things with physical properties than as symbols of moral and spiritual experiences. The heat, the thirst, the torture etc. are physical first and most obviously and symbolical at the secondary level, which is by no means less significant, so that the poem may be read and enjoyed as a story of a dangerous voyage pure and simple, before we delve deeper into its allegorical level. But in *The Waste Land* the familiar objects exist mostly on the symbolical plane, while the literal implication is kept throughout only as a continuous undercurrent.

The basic theme is set in motion by a human crime which is a sin in terms of its effect on the life and vitality of the human agent. In the *Rime* the crime is the killing of the Albatross, a creature of God, a guest of the sailors and the vital principle of life itself, as it later came to be associated with the good spirit that caused the wind to blow and the ship to move. In *The Waste Land* the sin of humanity lies in its total denial of God, the living fountain of its strength:

He who was living is now dead
We who were living now are dying
With a little patience.

The effect of Sin, in both the poems, is death, Coleridge conveys this idea in terms of sudden cessation of movement, with powerful rhythmic overtones:

Down dropt the breeze, the sails dropt down
't was sad as sad could be.
....
Day after day, day after day,
We stuck, nor breath, nor motion,
As idle as a painted ship upon a painted ocean,

This is an aspect of stalemate which Eliot presents in the second movement, life as a round of monotony and tedium without variety and further movement:

And we shall play the game of chess
Pressing lidless eyes, and waiting
For a knock at the door,

Sin as an inner degradation and decomposition of the spirit is reflected in the external surroundings, where death, decay, squalor, decomposition are writ large on all things. In Eliot the idea is elaborated and repeated so effectively that even an incurious reader cannot miss it. Coleridge is briefer but equally emphatic:

The very deep did rot, O Christ!
That ever this should be
Yea, slimy things did crawl with legs
Upon the slimy sea.

One is at once reminded of Eliot's dull canal and the rat dragging its slimy belly upon the vegetation and the dead bodies white and naked upon the low damp ground.

Then comes the description of the consequences of sin on the patient himself. We notice first the idea of the sinful creature or creatures under the curse of God. This idea is implied in Eliot's 'red-rock' as the vantage-point from which one can see 'fear in a handful of dust'. In the *Rime* the point is made quite explicit:

> But where the ship's dark shadow lay
> The charmed water burned alway
> A still and awful red.

The shadow under the red-rock also is still.

The motive of fear, which is indirectly conveyed in *The Waste Land* is elaborated and multiplied in *The Rime,* terror heaped upon terror on the sinner;

Thus fear sips at the heart-blood of the mariner, with the glazed eyes of dead men staring at him and the spectacle of the skeleton-boat and its ghostly crew advancing menacingly towards him:

> The night-mare life-in-death was she,
> Who thicks men's blood with cold.

The life-in-death motive is common to both the poems and in both it has a double dimension—it is at once hellish and purgatorial. In *The Waste Land* the protagonist watches the London crowd float over the bridge and is reminded of Dante's *Inferno*, 'I had not thought death had undone so many', and as he proceeds further he seems to hear the rattle of bones and 'the chuckle spread from ear to ear'. But in the final movement the suffering becomes almost purgatorial, a march through the universe of death towards the Chapel Perilous, the ultimate goal which has the promise of rebirth. In the *Rime* the mariner lives actually among the dead, whose eyes convey the implacable sense of curse:

> Seven days, seven nights, I saw that curse,
> And yet I could not die.

Then he becomes the victim of Life-in-Death and his remaining life is a prolonged purgatory.

Part of this curse is symbolized by the sterile heat of the burning sun, with no trace of water to slake the agonizing thirst. In *The Waste Land* the sun beats and the dead tree gives no shelter and dry stones no sound of water and the search for water later on becomes acute and frantic:

> But there is no water
> Sweat is dry and our feet
> Are in the sands.

In the *Rime* the idea is expressed with the same economy and incisiveness:

> All in a hot and copper sky,
> The bloody sun at noon
> Right up above the mast did stand
> No bigger than the moon
> ....
> Water, water, every where
> Nor any drop to drink
> ....
> And every tongue, through utter drought
> Was withered at the root.

In the fifth movement of *The Waste Land* the torment is intensified by the mocking sounds of spirits, which are mere illusions, will o' the wisps:

Red sullen faces sneer and snarl
From the doors of mud-cracked houses.

In the *Rime* the will o' the wisp is more immediate and not the less frightening because it is more concrete and real to the senses:

About, about, in reel and rout
The death fires danced at night;
The water like a witch's oils
Burnt green and blue and white.

But the most oppressive part of this experience is a sense of confinement, a living in a narrow prison without any sense of fellowship with aught in the surroundings. In *The Waste Land* this sense is conveyed by two powerful images: 'Rat's alley' and 'narrow garret' where dead men lost their bones, and secondly, 'we hear the key, each in his prison, thinking of the key each confirms the prison' etc. In *The Rime* this sense of isolation and confinement is unbearably immediate and oppressive: The mariner finds the hot sky pressing hard upon his burning lids, while the sea around is rotting and the dead lie at his feet. He wants to pray but his throat is choked.

Deliverance from this state is clearly suggested in *The Waste Land*, but fully worked out in the *Rime*. In this happy deliverance the moon replaces the sun and is followed by the showers of rain. The journey in the final part of *The Waste Land* ends with the arrival at the Chapel where in the moon-light the grass is singing, the cock is sounding its clarion, 'Co Co rico Co Co rico,' then 'damp gust bringing rain'. In the *Rime* also:

The rain poured down from one black cloud
The moon was at its edge.

The effect of this life-giving water of redemption is clear and unmistakable:

I was so light almost
I thought that I had died in sleep
And was a blessed ghost.

In *The Waste Land* the triple path of deliverance give, sympathize and control, stresses two crucial points. The first two terms in the formula emphasize the emotional release from the stranglehold of the ego, a sudden sally of the heart out of its own walls towards a conviction or commitment, 'the awful daring of a moment's surrender' or towards our fellow-creatures for close union and 'deeper communion', while the third combines the idea of release with that of inner discipline which serves only to regulate and ensure a smooth progress through the trials and the temptations of life, which is symbolized in 'the boat gliding gaily on the quiet surface of the sea'. In *The Rime* these stages are defined more clearly and concretely. The sense of 'give and sympathise', the sudden breaking through of the walls of the ego, is embodied in the spring of love which wells up in the heart of the mariner at the sight of the sea-snakes with their bright trails glittering in the moon-light:

A spring of love gushed from my heart
And I blessed them unaware.

The release is sudden and the 'painted ship' feels its impact and starts careering on its onward course:

Swiftly, swiftly flew the ship
Yet she sailed softly too.

In the closing part of *The Waste Land* Eliot hints at the line of personal purification and salvation in terms of the three fragments which he has shored against his ruin. They are accepted as the corner-stone of a personal philosophy wherein the greatest emphasis falls upon the willing acceptance of suffering as the purgatorial fire best calculated to ensure release and freedom from the burden of the senses and the sins peculiar to them. Coleridge's mariner is the best illustration of this idea; the process of redemption which starts spontaneously has to be completed and confirmed by suffering and penance which is practically life-long, and he wanders restlessly from place to place, driven by the compelling impulse to relieve himself by sharing his experiences with a fit person:

> I pass, like night, from land to land;
> I have strange power of speech;
> The moment that his face I see,
> I know the man that must hear me.

The third term in Eliot's formula refers to the sense of release arising from the complete destitution, a total freedom from all worldly attachments and common concerns of the normal men and women. The mariner is a living embodiment of this idea. He is physically close to the wedding-feast yet remains practically unconscious of it, a lonely abstracted creature, wrapped in the pall of dark thoughts and stopping others also from the eagerly-desired participation in the marriage festivities. Eliot indicates the nature of the impression such a person is likely to create on his fellow-beings, even when they come under his spell, in the apparently casual line, 'Hieronimo is mad again', which means that a person with profound spiritual experiences and suffering is apt to pass for a mad man with his complacent fellow-beings. The wedding-guest is a victim of this feeling or delusion:

> I fear thee, ancient Mariner;
> I fear thy skinny hand!
> And thou art long, and lank, and brown,
> As is the ribbed sea-sand.

The wedding-guest for all his opposition and resistance was compelled by the supernatural intensity of the mariner to listen to his talk and he returned home from this strange encounter 'a sadder and wiser man'. This phrase may be taken as the best brief summary of the effect of Eliot's poem on the heart and mind of all those who can play the 'wedding-guest' to the tale of modern life unfolded by his ghostly and deep-suffering figure, the blind, bisexual and all-seeing prophet of the human destiny, the protagonist, Tiresias. The final goal of Eliot's serious writings may also be summed up in the words of the mariner:

> O sweeter than the marriage-feast
> 'Ts sweeter far to me
> To walk together to the kirk
> With a goodly company
> To walk together to the kirk
> And all together pray,
> Old men, and babes, and loving friends
> And youths and maidens gay!

Diction and Versification: We have thus far discussed two salient features of the style in *The Waste Land*, the poetic short-hand and the employment of symbols and imagery as a deliberate device of indirect and highly economical, complex and suggestive statement of themes and ideas. We are now in a position to analyse more minutely and in greater detail Eliot's handling of language and his mastery over words and skill in combining them in a significant and artistic organization. From his critical pronouncements, quoted elsewhere, we can clearly understand Eliot's emphasis upon the poet's power of renewing and enriching the language, 'a shabby instrument constantly deteriorating' and his deliberate aim to avoid the conventional romantic tendency towards diffusion and exuberance with a decided preference for the colourful poetical words which had resulted in a cleavage between the poetic diction and the language of prose and the living speech actually spoken by men. The aim was to bridge the gulf between poetry and prose and vitalize the language of poetry through a generous infusion of the current, colloquial and apparently trite and unpoetical phraseology of the daily speech.

The diction in *The Waste Land* thus has three important elements: (*a*) The familiar words heightened and raised to the level of poetic intensity and suggestiveness. This element appears in the meditation of the protagonist; it dominates the opening and closing parts of the first section and practically the whole of the beautiful fourth movement and the major part of the final section; (*b*) The language of the common conversation scattered throughout the poem, where the diction is simple and unvarnished, yet the words and phrases conceal the art of fastidious selection...... 'common words exact without vulgarity'; (*c*) Quotations and echoes, direct or indirect, brief or elaborate, given separately or woven into the very texture of the sentences and paragraphs, where the aim is neither decorative nor pedantic, but always functional, the quotations and echoes are always pressed in the service of complexity and enrichment of the style. The words and phrases are not mechanically reproduced, but they are freely altered, modified and transformed, new-coined and stamped with new significance in the orginal context of the poem. We have already referred to the quotation from Webster, 'keep the wolf far thence that is enemy to man', changed into 'keep the dog far hence that is friend to man' etc. The alteration is drastic yet purposeful because the Dog becomes a symbol of re-birth and redemption, while ambivalently it re-inforces the destructive force which is already present in the 'wolf' of the original line. The quotations, as we have already shown, are part of an essential technique of 'parallelism and contrast', so necessary here for presenting the poet's sense of 'not only the pastness of the past, but also its presence'.

Eliot's use of language of all categories is marked by economy, precision and appropriateness. He would not use two epithets where only one can serve the purpose, but the one finally used will have the stamp of inevitability in the context, as well as a strong aura of association and suggestiveness. We have noted the explosive force of the word 'synthetic' in the description of Belladonna's luxury drawing-room and here note in passing other expressions of similar precision and wealth of assoeiation......'stirring dull roots', 'dull canal' 'lean solicitor' 'dirty ears', 'inviolable song' etc. We may also include under this head his effective use of vivid concrete and pictorial words which would have delighted T. E. Hulme, the Imagist. The fairest sample of this aspect is provided by the opening song of the Thames-daughters:

> The river sweats Oil and tar
> Barge. drift/Red sail Wide.

Eliot was definitely of the opinion that the meaning of a particular word is enriched by its meaning in other contexts of the same poem or in other works of the same author or of other writers. We have already illustrated this fact with reference to the word 'red' in 'red rock', 'torch light red on sweaty faces' and 'red sullen faces sneer and snarl'. Other examples are provided by 'like a taxi waiting, throbbing' of the female typist and Tiresias's 'throbbing between two lives'; the 'antique mantel' of Belladonna and the 'antique look' of poor Lil, 'hooded figure' and 'hooded hordes'; the 'nothing, nothing, nothing' of the mental life in the upper circle of the second movement and 'I can connect nothing with nothing' of the poor Thames-daughter. Examples may be multiplied and the point emphatically made that the use of the same word in different contexts can powerfully enrich its connotative force by implied comparison and contrast, provided by the contextual variations. From this we logically move to a simple but favourite device of Eliot for heightening the effect and significance of a single word. We have already glanced at a few illustrations of this device.........'Thinking, thinking, thinking' and 'nothing, nothing, nothing' in the second movement; burning, 'burning, burning' of the third; 'water, water, water' in the fifth and final section. The absence of peace and fertility is underlined by the repetition of the negative (no) in the opening section also:

> And the dead tree gives *no* shelter, the cricket *no* relief
> And dry stones *no* sound of water.

Great subtlety is shown by the poet in the handling of pronouns and the various tenses of a verb for effecting connections and combinations: Take, for example, the juxtaposition of past and present forms of the verbs in the following:

> 'And still she cried, and still the world pursues'

This is doing violence to the syntax in order to remove the barrier between the past and the present. Then, notice also the shift from singular to plural form of the personal pronoun:

> *I* have heard the key
> Turn in the door once and turn once only
> *We* think of the key each in his prison.

Apart from the symbolic use of common words—dog, bones, finger-nails and dirty hands etc.........to heighten their effect, the devices generally favoured by Eliot are paradox and ironic contrast. Thus

'April is the cruellest month and winter kept us warm'. In most cases the opposition is not verbal and so obvious, but runs through a whole passage of inner tension between two different ideas or contexts, one of the past and the other of the present. Thus, behind the 'cruellest April' of Eliot there lurks the spring with showers sweet of Chaucer; the dirty Thames and vulgar nymphs of to-day are ironically contrasted with the sweet Thames and pure nymphs of Spenser. We have already noticed the abrupt descent with powerful bathetic effect in such passages as 'when a lovely woman stoops to folly' and

> 'The moon shone bright on Mrs. Porter and her daughter
> They wash their feet in soda-water', etc.

Eliot enforces the effectiveness of an idea by means of abrupt reversal of the movement of a whole passage to a meaning diametrically opposed to what the reader has been induced to expect. Thus the opening lines in the final movement present the various steps, through the repetition of a series of 'after', leading to the final moment of Christ's Passion. But the last line veers suddenly from the death of Christ to 'He who was living is now dead'. Enough has now been said about Eliot's mastery over the language, his power of selecting the right and precise word and his subtle skill to combine them in such a way as to charge the familiar words with extraordinary intensity and suggestiveness.

Similar is the case with his manipulation of *rhythm and versification*, which is quite obviously characterized by variety, flexibility, mobility and extreme sensitiveness to the variations in emotional tone and intellectual tempo. The metre is always a part of the meaning and music enriches the sense through its powerful suggestive effect. Thus there is a running contrast between the slow, grave and majestic movement of the lines representing the meditation of Tiresias and the light, colloquial and informal ease clearly reflected in the conversation of the wastelanders. The very change in the rhythm is a forceful reminder of the transition from gravity to frivolity, from serious to the flippant plane of life. After the moving rhythm of 'April is the cruellest month' we come upon the jaunty rhythm of 'summer surprised us' to feel at once the shocking intrustion of the superficialities of the rootless and soulless humanity. At the crucial points the sense of contrast is most effectively suggested by the sudden change of rhythm. The most emphatic illustration is provided by the second movement where the external splendour and glamour of the lady are magnificently conveyed by the richness and grandeur of the verse movement, which, however, clashes violently with the nervous and broken ejaculations of the lady, and the clash vivifies the brittleness of her splendour and the disorganization of her inner life which that splendour can but ill conceal. In a subtler way the same sense of contrast is rhythmically conveyed in the passage which begins formally, but not without ironical overtone:

> But at my back from time to time I hear
> The sound of horns and motors—etc..

and then suddenly it descends to the ballad level in

O the moon shone bright on Mrs. Porter
And on her daugeer
They wash their feet in soda-water,

Even his onomatopoetic lines, apparently so conventional and unstriking, are made to serve an important function in their particular contexts. Thus, the passionate longing for water with the poignant sense of its absence—'If there were the sound of water only'.........is powerfully conveyed by the mimetic song of the hermit-thrush, 'Drip drop, drip drop, drop, drop, drop'. Similarly in same movement the trumpet notes of the crowing cock—'Co co rico co co rico'—actually enforces the effect of the end of confusion and darkness and the approach of morn and the moment of deliverance.

In the grave meditative passages themselves one can notice remarkable variations, in tone, rhythm and movement in response to the transitions in thought, feeling and mood. In the opening section, for example, the central passage starts on slow and emotionally subdued note:

What are the roots that clutch, what branches grow
Out of this stony rubbish ?

But the answer which follows has a mounting, almost breathless, movement which is clearly suggestive of the fervour of the speaker's conviction:

For you know only
A heap of broken images, where the sun beats,
And the dead tree gives no shelter, the cricket no relief
And the dry stone no sound of water.

We notice here the repetition of the emphatic negative (no, no, no) and the dying fall in the last line. In the crucial passage of the final movement the harmonious blending of music and meaning is quite obvious. The meaning of 'Datta' is conveyed in lines which appear to be 'shaking with blood':

> What have we given ?
> My friend, blood shaking my heart,
> The awful daring of a moment's surrender
> Which an age of prudence can never retract.

But this wave-like rhythm becomes broken, hesitant and poignantly repetitive in the passage following:

> I have heard the key
> Turn in the door once and turn once only
> We think of the key, each in his prison
> Thinking of the key, each confirms a prison.

In the third, the exhilarating sense of release is conveyed in the prolonged, emphatic and quietly confident tone and rhythm:

> The boat responded
> Gaily, to the hand expert with sail and oar
> The sea was calm, your heart would have responded
> Gaily, when invited, beating obedient
> To controlling hands.

In this way one may go on analysing and illustrating without exhausting the resources of Eliot's flexible rhythm and his skill in combining the lines of varying lengh, and words of different sounds, and tempo and pitch which have infinite shades of variation. He achieves the maximum of freedom without the least trace of incoherence or loss of control over the mobility of his verse.

The Charge of Obscurity: *The Waste Land* has been described by many a critic as an obscure poem, bristling with contorted lines and unintelligible passages and symbols. The charge is fairly sweeping and embraces the bulk of the modernist poetry. Eliot himself has noted the fact and offered an explanation for it, thrusting the burden of responsibility upon the unpoetical age.

> "The charge," he remarks, "has been brought against the more original literature of our time, that it has been written for a small and exclusive audience...... this is a consequence not of individual aberrancy but of social disintegration in the literary aspect of critical decay. It arises from a lack of continuous communication, of the artist with his friends and the fellow artists and the small number of keen amateures of arts, with a larger public educated in the same way, of taste cultivated upon the literature of the past, but ready to accept what is good in the present, when it is brought to their notice, and so with the world at large."

This is true as far as it goes, but it does not go far enough. The esoteric nature of the modernist literature arises generally from the technical complexity, verbal ingenuity and an allusiveness of style which tends to patronise out-of-the-way, obscure and specialized branch of learning.

We hasten, however, to add that *The Waste Land* is a difficult not an obscure poem. Once we acquire some insight into the intricacies of the mythical technique, its basic theme and the symbols and images, which, with a few exceptions, are not difficult to grasp, the poem will become substantially intelligible to us. Yet it is a difficult poem and the difficulty is studied and deliberate on the part of the poet. The most obvious factor responsible for this difficulty is the rigorous compression, which, we know, was dictated by Ezra Pound, 'the superior artist' as Eliot has called him, to whom the poem was submitted for scrutiny and who recommended a substantial reduction of its original size; the result is that all the sign-posts which a poet generally erects to guide the readers into the heart of his meaning have been ruthlessly removed and the reader is faced with a veritable labyrinth without the thread to show the way out. we do not know who is speaking to whom and on what occasion. It is a poem without plot and hero and without a clear logical li nk between one step and another. The complex type of the interior monologue which the poet adapts to the requirements of this orchestral poem relies upon the free association of ideas and mental jumps which leave the reader breathless and confused. No wonder, therefore, that he is disposed, in utter disgust, to exclaim that it is all a babel of tongues, the ravings of a set of maniacs.

Then there is the allusiveness of the style with its extraordinarily wide range, comprehending several literatures and cultures and fields other than literary, such as anthropology, religion and philosophy. Allusiveness, however, has always been a salient feature of poetry and an erudite and scholarly poet writes under the clear conviction that his meaning can be grasped only by the few—fit audience and few—and it will be the final 'reward' of consummate scholarship. Yet even in the case of a poet as learned as Milton, the tracing of the quotations and allusions to their sources will pave the way for an easy understanding of the poet's thought and meaning. But in *The Waste Land* the problem is more complex. Here the poet takes a certain extract from an old author, say Webster, alters its key word and uses the modified line in his own context... 'keep the Dog far hence'--and thus makes the meaning practically independent of the original quotation. There are numerous echoes of the Bible, of Shakespeare, Dante, Baudelaire, Joyce etc. but their bearings on the context in the poem are complex, oblique, often ironical and certainly hard to grasp by even the fairly educated reader.

Eliot's indirect method and the scrupulous avoidance of direct statement, and adoption of the symbolic medium contribute their share to the difficulty of the poem. We are never sure of the poet's own thought and feelings and his symbols being not only complex but ambivalent the reader has to fall back upon his own resources to understand and interpret the poem without any hope that his understanding of the poem is right and it will be shared by other readers and critics. These and many other peculiarities of the poem have conspired to make it extremely difficult for the average reader. Eliot wrote it under the conviction that the poet of a complex and confused age is bound to be difficult, allusive and even obscure, a conviction which was confirmed by the attitude of his mentor, Ezra Pound, and the practice of his favourite authors, the English Metaphysicals and the French symbolists. But the technique which he cultivated in this poem was only a passing phase and in his later poetry, where he withdrew into his private world, he gave up this manner and developed a style more responsive to his personal, authentic voice, turning the corrugated surface into something smooth and transparent and moving from knotted complexity into the purity of deeper intensisy. This, however, is not a condemnation of the technique in *The Waste Land* which suits the intention of the poet to a nicety. He started with the object of inter-weaving the parts of several cultures into an intelligible whole, of telescoping the past and the present in a scheme of harmonious tension and putting together what other poets and thinkers have said about the godless humanity, and he devised a technique, which, with all its limitations, is a monument to his artistic skill, his power of organization and his unsurpassed mastery over the meaning and the music of words. It has been said that in the poetry of the great technicians of verse like Ezra Pound and Auden a mountain of labour is required to get at the meaning which, like the proverbial Quaker's horse, is difficult to catch and good-for-nothing if finally caught. The reader of *The Waste Land*, however, will never fail to find his labour amply rewarded by the solid gold of profound wisdom at the core and a feast of perpetual delight to his intellect and aesthetic sensibility on the verbal surface—so various, so new, so rich and so vivid.

The poet himself has provided the key to the comprehension of this and other symbolic poems in the remark that the reader should allow the images and symbols to sink into his mind, where they should remain and gradually blend and combine into a coherent whole. We have already referred to the phrase of I. A. Richards, 'the music of ideas', which among other things, serves to endorse the view of Eliot. So we should first fix upon the general sense with the help of images and symbols and then gradually pass to the particular details. The poetry of Eliot thus demands a life-long communion, which he himself recommends to the students of Dante:

> "The majority of poems one outgrows and outlives, as one outgrows and outlives the majority of human passions: Dante's is one of those which one can only just hope to grow up to at the end of life".

Like Dante Eliot is the poet of the men of cultivated taste and adult mind who go to poetry not for momentary intoxication or 'dull opiate' to forget the wounds inflicted by life, but for deeper wisdom and insight and for the cultivation of that profound tragic vision, which, according to W. B. Yeats, is the hall-mark of the maturity of mind, heart and imagination.

INDEX